AF673209

Leading Through Crisis

Case Studies on Crisis Management

Gerard Assey

Leading Through Crisis: Case Studies on Crisis Management

By
Gerard Assey

© Copyright 2025 by Author

Published by:
Gerard Assey
19/18, Palli Arasan Street
Anna Nagar East
Chennai - 600 102

ISBN: 978-81-989262-0-3

All Rights Reserved. No part of this publication may be reproduced, stored in a retrieval system, or transmitted in any form or by any means- electronic or mechanical, including photocopying, recording, or by any information storage and retrieval system, without prior written permission from the author.

(Cover Courtesy: Image by redgreystock on Freepik)

Table of Contents

Disclaimer

This book is a work of professional insight and reflection intended for educational and developmental purposes. All case studies, scenarios, names of individuals, organizations, and locations presented herein are entirely fictitious and have been carefully crafted to illustrate various aspects of crisis management. Any resemblance to actual persons, living or dead, or to real companies, institutions, events, or places is purely coincidental and unintentional. The examples are designed to provoke thought, encourage strategic discussion, and facilitate learning. No part of this book should be interpreted as referencing or representing any real-life business or individual unless explicitly stated. Readers are encouraged to apply the concepts within with discretion and adapt them to their unique contexts and environments.

Introduction

In an increasingly unpredictable and volatile world, organizations and their leaders are constantly facing crises that can threaten the stability and future of their businesses. Whether it's a financial downturn, a reputational disaster, or an operational failure, crises are inevitable. In recent years, we've seen a surge in unforeseen global events that have left many businesses and leaders struggling to stay afloat—such as economic recessions, the COVID-19 pandemic, cyber-attacks, and major disruptions to global supply chains. The speed at which crises emerge and the complexity with which they manifest requires leaders to be more adaptable, informed, and proactive than ever before.

The core purpose of this book is to serve as a comprehensive guide for leaders—CEOs, C-suite executives, and senior managers—on how to navigate crises effectively. This book not only provides theoretical knowledge but offers a practical, hands-on approach to crisis management by presenting detailed case studies and real-life scenarios that leaders can learn from. These case studies will showcase both the successes and failures of crisis management, offering valuable insights into how leaders can steer their organizations through the storm and emerge stronger on the other side.

Through a structured approach to crisis management, this book addresses the urgent need for leaders to be better prepared. Whether you are faced with financial instability, a public relations nightmare, or a sudden operational breakdown, the lessons and tools provided here will give you the confidence and strategies to manage any crisis and lead your organization to success. In a time where the only constant is change, this book will help you become a resilient, adaptable, and decisive leader.

The Role of Leaders in Crisis: Overview of Leadership Roles During Crises

Leadership in times of crisis is distinctly different from leadership in normal times. When an organization is running smoothly, the role of a leader is to guide, strategize, and grow the business. However, during a crisis, the dynamics shift significantly. Leaders become the linchpins holding the organization together. Their ability to act swiftly, communicate effectively, and make difficult decisions often determines whether the organization will survive the crisis or collapse under its weight.

At the core, a leader in crisis must exhibit a unique blend of traits: decisiveness, empathy, resilience, and vision. Leaders are expected to maintain calm under pressure, inspire confidence in their teams, and provide clear direction amidst chaos. Employees, stakeholders, and the public look to leaders for reassurance and guidance, which places an enormous responsibility on their shoulders. A crisis does not simply test the organization's capacity to recover but also challenges a leader's character and decision-making abilities.

Consider the case of Jonathan Westfield, CEO of a mid-sized manufacturing company, Stratford Machines, which faced a sudden and catastrophic supply chain failure. Key components from their international supplier were delayed indefinitely due to a political upheaval in the supplier's country. With orders piling up and customers demanding explanations, Jonathan was thrown into a high-pressure situation with no clear end in sight. He could either panic or lead. Recognizing the magnitude of the crisis, Jonathan immediately assembled his senior leadership team and began formulating a contingency plan. His ability to stay composed, think critically, and delegate tasks efficiently allowed Stratford Machines to pivot to an alternative supplier within two weeks. Although the disruption caused a short-term delay, the company was able to fulfill its contracts with minimal damage to its reputation. Jonathan's leadership not only stabilized the company during the crisis but also earned him the trust and respect of his team, who witnessed firsthand how effective crisis management looks in action.

This example highlights the pivotal role of leaders during crises. It is not enough to merely react to a crisis—leaders must anticipate challenges, communicate transparently, and make informed decisions that minimize damage and ensure long-term success. This book will delve into many more such examples, shedding light on the various ways leaders can stand out in the face of adversity.

Importance of Case Studies: How Case Studies Help Train Leaders and Managers in Real-Life Problem-Solving and Decision-Making

Case studies have long been recognized as one of the most powerful tools for training professionals, particularly leaders and managers who are required to make high-stakes decisions. The effectiveness of case studies lies in their ability to simulate real-life scenarios, forcing individuals to think critically, analyze complex situations, and consider multiple variables before arriving at a decision. Unlike theoretical lessons that often fail to capture the nuances of real-world situations, case studies provide a hands-on learning experience that equips leaders with practical skills they can apply in their daily roles.

Consider the analogy of a pilot being trained in a flight simulator. While books and lectures can teach the mechanics of flying, nothing prepares a pilot for an emergency like the immersive experience of a simulated crisis. The same principle applies to leadership in crisis management. Reading about crisis management theories is valuable, but working through detailed case studies allows leaders to practice applying those theories in situations that closely mirror real-life crises.

For example, one of the case studies in this book explores the financial collapse of Nimbus Electronics, a tech startup that expanded too rapidly and found itself unable to cover its operational costs. The case study walks through how Nimbus' CFO, Emily Forester, managed to secure emergency funding while negotiating with creditors to avoid bankruptcy. Readers are prompted to analyze Emily's decision-making process, weigh the options she had at each stage of the crisis, and critique her approach. Was there a better way she could have handled the situation? What would you have done differently in her shoes?

By engaging with these kinds of case studies, leaders and managers can hone their problem-solving skills in a safe environment, where the consequences of making the wrong choice are minimal. This prepares them to make better decisions when they are inevitably faced with crises in their own organizations. Moreover, case studies foster discussion and collaboration among leadership teams, allowing them to explore different perspectives and approaches to problem-solving.

Throughout this book, case studies are used not just as storytelling devices, but as interactive tools that challenge readers to think like crisis leaders. Each case study concludes with reflective questions and exercises, designed to deepen the reader's understanding of the crisis and the decisions made. Whether used in individual learning or group training sessions, these case studies will serve as powerful tools for leaders looking to sharpen their crisis management skills.

How to Use This Book: Guidance on Using the Case Studies, Templates, and Frameworks for Maximum Impact

This book is designed to be both informative and practical. It is not just a collection of crisis management theories or leadership philosophies, but a hands-on guide that provides actionable insights, tools, and strategies for navigating crises. To ensure you get the most out of this book, here are a few ways you can approach it:

- ✓ **Case Study Immersion**: Each chapter presents a detailed case study that highlights a different aspect of crisis management, whether it's financial, reputational, or operational. As you read these case studies, immerse yourself in the scenario. Put yourself in the shoes of the leaders and managers involved. Ask yourself, "What would I do?" Reflect on the decisions made, and think critically about how you might handle a similar situation in your own organization.

- ✓ **Templates and Tools**: Throughout the book, you will find templates and frameworks designed to guide you through key aspects of crisis management—such as crisis communication plans, scenario planning exercises, and decision-making frameworks. These tools are meant to be immediately applicable to your organization. Don't just read them—use them. Modify these templates to fit the specific needs of your team or business. Practice filling out a scenario plan for a potential crisis your organization could face in the future. These tools are intended to serve as living documents that evolve with your business.
- ✓ **Collaborative Learning**: While this book can be read individually, it is highly recommended that leaders use it as a collaborative learning resource with their management teams. Gather your senior leadership team and discuss the case studies together. Compare different perspectives on how crises should be handled. You will be surprised at how much collective wisdom emerges from these discussions, and how much you can learn from one another.
- ✓ **Reflection and Application**: After reading each chapter, take time to reflect on the key takeaways and how they apply to your own leadership style. What are the gaps in your current crisis management approach? How can you implement the lessons learned into your organization's crisis preparedness plans?

The goal of this book is not just to provide knowledge, but to inspire action. Use it as a roadmap to build confidence in your crisis management abilities and to better prepare your organization for the inevitable challenges ahead.

By approaching this book with an open mind and a willingness to engage with the material, you will be well-equipped to handle whatever crises come your way. Whether you are a CEO steering your company through turbulent waters, or a senior executive looking to fortify your leadership team's crisis response, the lessons, case studies, and tools in this book will help you become a more confident and effective leader.

This introduction sets the stage for the rest of the book, emphasizing why crisis management is critical in today's business environment and how the structured approach presented in the subsequent chapters will provide leaders with practical tools to navigate any crisis they may face.

Part 1:
Understanding Crisis Management

Chapter 1: What is Crisis Management?

Crisis management is one of the most vital aspects of leadership today. In a world where disruptions occur at an alarming rate, ranging from financial meltdowns and environmental disasters to operational failures and reputational crises, organizations need to be prepared. Understanding crisis management is not just about dealing with challenges as they arise but about proactively recognizing potential threats and having strategies in place to mitigate their impact. This chapter will explore the essence of crisis management, examine various types of crises, define the role of leaders during these turbulent times, and explain why crises happen, differentiating between internal and external factors.

Defining Crisis: Types of Crises

A crisis is any unexpected event that disrupts normal operations and poses a threat to an organization's well-being, reputation, or survival. Crises often strike without warning, challenging the organization's ability to respond quickly and effectively. They can take various forms, each presenting unique challenges.

Financial Crises

Financial crises are among the most destructive types of crises, impacting the very foundation of an organization. When a company faces severe financial difficulties—such as insolvency, massive debt, or plummeting revenue—leadership is tested to the core. A financial crisis doesn't just threaten profitability; it can erode stakeholder confidence, damage the company's reputation, and lead to layoffs or even closure.

Consider the case of Bryson Dynamics, a high-tech manufacturing firm. In 2018, Bryson found itself teetering on the edge of bankruptcy due to a poorly timed expansion into international markets. The financial crisis was exacerbated when the company's main product line became obsolete due to advancements in technology that they had failed to anticipate. Marcus Taylor, the CEO, realized that they were facing a collapse that could bring down the entire company if immediate action wasn't taken. In a desperate attempt to stay afloat, Marcus restructured the company, closing unprofitable divisions and refocusing efforts on a new, cutting-edge product. By securing emergency financing and taking drastic cost-cutting measures, Marcus was able to steer Bryson Dynamics back from the brink, but not without substantial losses. This case illustrates how a financial crisis, if mishandled, can lead to catastrophic failure, but if managed well, can lead to transformation and survival.

Reputational Crises

A reputational crisis occurs when an organization's public image is damaged, often due to scandals, product failures, ethical lapses, or poor customer service. Such crises can erode trust, leading to customer losses, a decline in market share, and lasting brand damage.

In 2021, Nelson & Stone, a luxury hotel chain, found itself in the midst of a reputational crisis when reports surfaced about unhygienic conditions and improper handling of COVID-19 protocols at one of its flagship locations. The issue quickly went viral, with social media platforms and news outlets amplifying the negative publicity. The CEO, Charlotte Nelson, faced a barrage of criticism and saw bookings drop by 40% in a single week. To manage the reputational crisis, Charlotte immediately issued a public apology, launched an internal investigation, and implemented stricter health and safety measures across all hotel locations. Moreover, she invited customers to engage with the company on social media, sharing their concerns and offering suggestions for improvement. Within six months, Nelson & Stone managed to restore some of its lost reputation, but the crisis served as a stark reminder of how fragile trust can be, and how critical it is for leaders to act transparently during reputational crises.

Operational Crises

Operational crises occur when an organization experiences a breakdown in its day-to-day operations. This can result from system failures, supply chain disruptions, workplace accidents, or human errors. Operational crises often have a direct and immediate impact on the organization's ability to serve its customers, which can lead to long-term damage if not managed swiftly.

An example of an operational crisis occurred at Vertex Logistics, a large shipping company that prided itself on punctuality. In early 2020, a sudden failure in their automated dispatch system caused major delays, leaving hundreds of shipments stranded across several countries. The crisis worsened when frustrated clients began pulling their business and switching to competitors. David Reynolds, the COO, quickly assembled a task force to address the issue. He not only had the system fixed but also initiated a manual backup protocol to prevent future failures. Vertex managed to recover, but not without losing key contracts, demonstrating that operational crises, if not handled quickly and efficiently, can severely damage a company's standing in the market.

Environmental Crises

Environmental crises stem from natural disasters or events that are outside the organization's control, such as hurricanes, earthquakes, floods, or pandemics. These crises often have widespread consequences and require an organization to not only manage its own recovery but also assist its employees and customers in coping with the aftermath.

When Oakridge Manufacturing, a company that produced eco-friendly packaging, was hit by a major flood in 2019, it saw its production facility submerged in several feet of water. The CEO, Linda Rivera, had to act fast. With most of her workforce displaced and key machinery damaged, the crisis seemed insurmountable. However, Linda's foresight in disaster preparedness, which included detailed emergency response plans and insurance policies, allowed the company to recover more swiftly than expected. Within three months, Oakridge was fully operational again, with a renewed focus on resilience in the face of environmental crises. Linda's leadership during the crisis not only saved the company but also earned her respect from the community and the workforce.

These examples illustrate that crises come in many forms and require unique responses. No organization is immune, and it is the responsibility of leadership to ensure that they are prepared for any eventuality.

The Leader's Role in Crisis: What Differentiates Successful Leaders During Crises?

While crises vary in their nature and severity, one constant is the importance of strong leadership. The leader's role during a crisis is fundamentally different from their role during normal times. In a crisis, leaders are expected to not only manage the immediate fallout but to inspire confidence and provide a clear path forward. What differentiates successful leaders during crises?

- ✓ **Decisiveness and Speed**: Leaders must make quick decisions based on incomplete information. Indecision can exacerbate the crisis, leading to paralysis within the organization. Successful leaders understand that waiting for perfect information is a luxury they don't have during a crisis.

  Take the example of Lucinda Hart, the CEO of Phoenix Apparel, a clothing company hit hard by a major supply chain disruption during a global pandemic. Lucinda didn't wait for the situation to fully unravel before taking action. Within hours of learning about the disruption, she reached out to alternative suppliers, developed a contingency plan, and communicated transparently with her customers about potential delays. Her ability to act quickly helped mitigate the impact on the company's operations and reassured customers that Phoenix Apparel was doing everything in its power to meet their needs.
- ✓ **Communication and Transparency**: In times of crisis, effective communication is essential. Leaders must communicate clearly and frequently with stakeholders, employees, and

the public, providing updates on the crisis and steps being taken to resolve it. Transparency helps build trust and prevents rumors and misinformation from spreading.

When Eastern Airlines faced a public relations crisis after a mid-flight emergency landing was mishandled by the crew, CEO Robert Daniels took to the airwaves immediately. He didn't wait for the full details to emerge; instead, he issued a public apology, reassured the public that an investigation was underway, and communicated directly with the passengers involved. His transparency helped prevent the crisis from escalating further and demonstrated a level of accountability that restored confidence in the airline.

- ✓ **Resilience and Emotional Intelligence**: Successful leaders during crises exhibit resilience and emotional intelligence. They must remain calm under pressure, absorb the stress of the situation without passing it onto their teams, and demonstrate empathy for those affected by the crisis. Emotional intelligence helps leaders understand the emotional toll that a crisis can take on their employees, customers, and stakeholders.

  In the case of Ivy Tech Solutions, a software company that faced a massive data breach, CEO Nathaniel Boone was visibly shaken by the crisis. But instead of panicking, he focused on supporting his team emotionally. He held daily check-ins with his employees, offering reassurance and listening to their concerns. His empathy and calm demeanor helped his employees stay focused on the task at hand—

mitigating the breach and securing customer data.

Leaders who can navigate these elements—decisiveness, communication, and emotional intelligence—are more likely to successfully guide their organizations through crises.

Why Crises Happen: Internal vs. External Factors

Crises can arise from a multitude of factors, and it is essential for leaders to understand the root causes. Broadly speaking, crises can be divided into two categories: internal and external.

Internal Factors

Internal crises are those that arise from within the organization. These could stem from leadership failures, poor financial management, operational inefficiencies, or internal conflict. Internal crises are often the result of organizational vulnerabilities that have been ignored or poorly managed over time.

For example, the downfall of Finster Foods, a regional grocery chain, was largely due to poor financial management. The company expanded too quickly without adequate capital reserves, and when sales began to decline, Finster found itself unable to pay its suppliers. The crisis was compounded by weak leadership that failed to recognize the warning signs. In this case, the internal financial mismanagement was the root cause of the crisis.

External Factors

External crises are triggered by factors outside the organization's control. These could include natural disasters, economic downturns, geopolitical events, or changes in market conditions. External crises often require organizations to adapt rapidly to changing circumstances and implement contingency plans.

A clear example of an external crisis is the Blum Energy Company. In 2020, the company was severely affected by new government regulations that restricted the use of non-renewable energy sources. These regulations, which had been in the pipeline for years, hit Blum Energy harder than most because they had not diversified their energy portfolio in time. While the external factor was the new regulation, the company's slow adaptation to changing market conditions worsened the crisis.

In both cases, whether internal or external, crises underscore the importance of organizational agility and preparedness. Leaders who understand the source of the crisis can respond more effectively, mitigating the damage and guiding their organizations to recovery.

In conclusion, crisis management is a critical skill for any leader, requiring a blend of strategic decision-making, clear communication, emotional intelligence, and an understanding of the internal and external factors that contribute to crises. As we continue through this book, we will delve deeper into strategies and frameworks that leaders can use to effectively manage crises and emerge stronger on the other side. The key takeaway from this chapter is that crises, while inevitable, do not have to spell disaster. With the right preparation, response, and leadership, crises can become opportunities for transformation and growth.

Chapter 2:
The Importance of Case Studies as a Training Tool

In leadership development, one of the most powerful tools available is the use of case studies. Unlike traditional teaching methods, case studies allow leaders to engage with real-world problems in a way that fosters critical thinking, problem-solving, and decision-making. CEOs, executives, and managers benefit from this hands-on approach because it simulates real-life situations, encouraging them to think deeply and reflect on their actions. In this chapter, we will explore the benefits of using case studies in leadership training, how they effectively mimic real-life scenarios, and how trainers and coaches can incorporate them into leadership development programs for maximum impact.

Benefits of Using Case Studies for Training CEOs, Executives, and Managers

Training top-level executives—CEOs, managers, and decision-makers—requires methods that go beyond theoretical knowledge. These individuals are tasked with making high-stakes decisions, often under extreme pressure and with incomplete information. The use of case studies in their training provides a unique advantage because it closely mirrors the unpredictable nature of real-world leadership challenges.

One of the primary benefits of using case studies is that they place leaders in situations that require immediate, thoughtful responses. A theoretical discussion about crisis management might help leaders understand the key principles, but a case study pushes them to apply those principles under realistic constraints, such as time pressure, conflicting interests, and limited resources. Leaders are challenged to make decisions, and these decisions are then scrutinized, allowing for reflection and learning.

Consider the fictional case of Brightview Technologies, a mid-sized company that specialized in developing smart home products. The CEO, Liam Stevens, had led the company through rapid growth, but in 2023, they faced a sudden downturn. A significant data breach exposed customer information, leading to a reputational crisis that saw their stock price drop by 35% in a single week. Competitors took advantage of Brightview's vulnerability, and the media portrayed the company as untrustworthy.

A case study of Brightview's response would ask trainees to step into Liam's shoes. How should he respond to the media? What actions could restore customer trust? Should Brightview issue refunds, offer public apologies, or take a different approach? These types of questions force executives to navigate through difficult decisions, considering financial implications, ethical responsibilities, and long-term brand impact. By analyzing this scenario, CEOs and executives not only learn how Liam handled the situation but also explore what alternative strategies could have been employed.

Another benefit is the emotional engagement case studies provide. When leaders read about actual companies facing serious challenges, they feel a sense of responsibility. They often experience a rush of emotions, such as anxiety, empathy, or frustration, which are essential in mimicking the emotional realities they will face in their own leadership roles. This engagement leads to deeper learning, as leaders are not just intellectually processing the information but are emotionally invested in the outcomes of the decisions they would make.

How Case Studies Mimic Real-Life Scenarios to Provide Practical Learning

The beauty of case studies lies in their ability to replicate the complexity and unpredictability of real-world leadership challenges. Unlike simple problem-solving exercises that present straightforward issues, case studies throw leaders into the chaotic world of ambiguity. This is where practical learning comes into play.

In real life, decisions often have ripple effects, influencing not just the immediate situation but the broader ecosystem of stakeholders, including employees, customers, shareholders, and the community. Case studies simulate this dynamic by presenting complex, multi-layered problems. Leaders are rarely given all the information they need upfront. Instead, they must sift through data, prioritize competing demands, and anticipate long-term consequences.

Let's look at another example involving Hudson Innovations, a fictional start-up that developed eco-friendly water filtration systems. In 2021, Hudson launched a new product that was initially met with praise for its innovative technology and sustainable approach. However, after several customers reported health issues potentially linked to the product, the company was thrust into a crisis. Was it a manufacturing defect, or was there misinformation spreading among consumers? Should the company issue a recall, which would cost millions, or continue investigating before taking action?

A case study based on this situation could force executives to explore multiple angles:

- ✓ What immediate steps should the CEO and leadership team take to investigate the claims?
- ✓ Should they address the public through social media, or would that escalate the issue prematurely?
- ✓ What are the ethical considerations if further health reports emerge?

By simulating real-life crises, case studies challenge leaders to make quick decisions with far-reaching consequences. They encourage practical learning by allowing individuals to see how theoretical principles—such as crisis communication, ethical decision-making, and stakeholder management—apply in practice. More importantly, they reveal the complexity of leadership. There are no "perfect" answers, just trade-offs, and leaders must learn to navigate these uncertainties.

To make this learning even more effective, case studies often end with a "what happened next" section, providing the real-life outcome of the crisis (or in fictional cases, a plausible ending). This feedback allows executives to reflect on their decisions and compare them to what others have done in similar situations. They can identify what worked, what didn't, and why, leading to a deeper understanding of the skills required in leadership.

How Trainers and Coaches Can Incorporate Case Studies into Leadership Development Programs

Incorporating case studies into leadership development programs is both an art and a science. Trainers and coaches must select the right case studies, structure discussions effectively, and guide participants toward meaningful insights. Here are some best practices for integrating case studies into leadership training:

- ✓ **Selecting Relevant Case Studies**

  The first step is choosing case studies that are relevant to the participants. A case study on crisis management, for example, might resonate more with senior executives than with mid-level managers, who may be more focused on day-to-day operational issues. Likewise, industry-specific case studies can help participants connect the scenarios to their own experiences.

  For instance, when training senior managers at Lakeshore Pharmaceuticals, a fictional company specializing in biotech innovation, the trainer used a case study about a real-life pharmaceutical recall that dealt with FDA regulations, public relations nightmares, and internal management conflicts. Participants were encouraged to dissect the various layers of decision-making, regulatory compliance, and public perception. By choosing a case study in their field, the trainer ensured that participants could immediately relate to the issues at hand.

- ✓ **Facilitating Group Discussions**

  Case studies work best when used as a platform for group discussions. Trainers should create an environment where participants can openly share their thoughts and challenge one another's perspectives. In a case study about ethical leadership, for instance, one participant might argue for transparency at all costs, while another might advocate for a more cautious, internally focused approach. These debates mirror the discussions that executives have in the real world and provide a safe space for testing ideas.

For example, in a workshop for managers at Stonebridge Automotive, a fictional auto parts manufacturer, the case study involved a supplier that was caught using substandard materials, leading to a large recall of defective parts. The group was divided into teams and asked to propose different courses of action. One team suggested immediately terminating the supplier relationship and issuing a public apology, while another team recommended quietly fixing the issue to avoid negative press. This exercise allowed the managers to see the strengths and weaknesses of each approach and understand the nuanced decision-making process in a real-world crisis.

- ✓ **Using Role-Playing to Enhance Engagement**

  To deepen the learning experience, trainers can incorporate role-playing as part of the case study. Participants can be assigned roles within the case, such as CEO, CFO, or Head of Public Relations, and asked to make decisions from that perspective. This not only increases engagement but helps participants appreciate the different responsibilities and pressures that each role brings during a crisis. In the case of MossGreen Financial, a fictional investment firm embroiled in a regulatory scandal, participants took on roles such as Chief Legal Officer, Head of Compliance, and CEO. Each person was given a unique set of priorities to balance, such as protecting the firm's reputation, avoiding legal ramifications, and maintaining client trust. By simulating real-life roles, participants gained a deeper understanding of the diverse pressures that influence decision-making during crises.

✓ **Reflection and Feedback**

After working through the case study, trainers should facilitate a period of reflection where participants can evaluate their decisions and compare them to what others in similar situations have done. This reflection phase is critical for identifying lessons learned and ensuring that the insights gained are translated into actionable strategies.

At the end of a case study workshop for executives at Evergreen Global, a fictional energy company dealing with a public relations crisis after an oil spill, the participants were asked to reflect on what they had learned about handling environmental disasters. Some realized that they had underestimated the power of community engagement in crisis recovery, while others recognized the importance of aligning corporate values with public messaging. This reflection process solidified the learning and prepared them for similar challenges in the future.

In conclusion, case studies are invaluable tools in leadership development programs, offering practical, real-world scenarios that challenge CEOs, executives, and managers to think critically, make tough decisions, and learn from their mistakes. By mimicking the complexities of real-life situations, case studies help leaders develop the skills they need to navigate crises, manage stakeholders, and lead their organizations effectively. Trainers and coaches who incorporate case studies into their programs create a dynamic learning environment where participants not only gain knowledge but also develop the confidence to lead in times of uncertainty.

Chapter 3:
How to Use Case Studies in Training

In leadership development, the impact of case studies hinges on their structure and how effectively they engage participants in learning. Case studies are not simply stories to be read and analyzed; they are immersive experiences designed to simulate real-world challenges, encouraging leaders to navigate the complexity of decision-making, problem-solving, and collaboration. This chapter will explore how to structure a case study for maximum learning impact, how to engage management teams with scenario-based exercises, and how case studies foster critical skills such as decision-making and collaboration.

Structuring a Case Study for Effective Learning

The success of any case study depends heavily on how it is structured. A well-structured case study isn't merely a recount of events; it's a tool designed to guide participants through the complexities of a scenario, encouraging them to critically assess each aspect of the situation.

1. Clear Objectives

The first step in structuring a case study is to define its learning objectives. For example, if the goal is to enhance decision-making skills in crisis management, the case study should be built around a scenario that forces participants to make difficult decisions under pressure. Alternatively, if the focus is on team collaboration, the case should introduce a multi-layered problem that requires different stakeholders to work together to find a solution.

Example: In the fictional company Nexus Solutions, the CEO, Rachel Garcia, faces a dilemma. A whistleblower has come forward with evidence that the company's manufacturing process is emitting harmful chemicals, violating environmental laws. Nexus Solutions is on the verge of a major IPO, and this news could derail the process, tanking their market valuation. The case study's objective is to challenge participants to navigate ethical decision-making, crisis communication, and legal strategy, balancing the need for transparency with the financial implications of the IPO.

2. Realistic Complexity

For the case study to be effective, it must reflect the complexity of real-world situations. Crises, in particular, rarely have one clear solution. There are multiple stakeholders with competing interests, and decisions often have long-term consequences that are difficult to foresee. The case study should simulate these dynamics by introducing incomplete information, unexpected developments, and pressure from various stakeholders.

In the Nexus Solutions case, participants must weigh the short-term financial losses of delaying the IPO against the long-term damage to the company's reputation and the legal risks of hiding the violation. Additional layers of complexity might include pressure from investors to move forward with the IPO or conflicting reports from internal departments about the severity of the environmental impact. These variables force participants to think critically and adapt to changing circumstances.

3. Decision Points

Effective case studies include multiple decision points, where participants must make critical choices based on the information provided. These decision points should not have clear right or wrong answers, but rather, they should force participants to explore the trade-offs between different courses of action. By doing this, participants are encouraged to reflect on their decision-making process and consider alternative strategies.

In the Nexus Solutions case, the first decision point might involve whether to inform the public about the potential environmental violations before the IPO. Should the company issue a press release to maintain transparency, or should they work behind the scenes to resolve the issue before it becomes public? Each decision point presents an opportunity for participants to engage in discussions, evaluate options, and learn from their choices.

Engaging Management Teams with Scenario-Based Exercises

Case studies are most effective when they actively engage participants in the problem-solving process. Rather than passively reading through a scenario, participants should be drawn into the situation and asked to role-play, collaborate, and debate potential solutions. Scenario-based exercises are a powerful way to achieve this.

1. Role-Playing for Perspective

One of the most engaging ways to use case studies is through role-playing. By assigning participants specific roles within the scenario, such as CEO, CFO, or Head of Public Relations, trainers can help participants step into the shoes of key decision-makers. This not only increases engagement but also helps leaders appreciate the different perspectives and pressures that come with each role.

Example: In the Nexus Solutions case, participants can be divided into teams representing different stakeholders: senior executives, legal counsel, investors, and environmental advocates. Each group has its own set of priorities—executives want to preserve the IPO timeline, legal counsel is concerned about regulatory compliance, and environmental advocates demand transparency. The role-playing exercise forces participants to navigate these competing interests, debate strategies, and work toward a consensus.

2. Simulating Real-Time Decision-Making

In real life, crises unfold in real time, with new information constantly emerging. Trainers can simulate this dynamic by introducing new developments at key moments during the case study exercise. For instance, just as the participants in the Nexus Solutions case agree on a strategy, the trainer could introduce an unexpected complication, such as a news leak about the environmental violation. This creates urgency and requires participants to adjust their plans quickly.

These real-time updates mimic the unpredictability of leadership in crisis situations and push participants to think on their feet. By creating a sense of immediacy, trainers can encourage leaders to practice decision-making under pressure, a critical skill in any leadership role.

3. Group Collaboration and Debate

Effective leaders must be able to work collaboratively, listening to others' viewpoints and making decisions that incorporate diverse perspectives. Case studies that involve group work promote this by encouraging participants to debate strategies and defend their positions. Structured group discussions foster critical thinking and challenge participants to back up their decisions with sound reasoning.

In the Nexus Solutions case, participants might be asked to present their strategy for managing the crisis to the rest of the group, defending their decisions on transparency, legal risk, and financial impact. The group can then engage in a debate, challenging one another on the trade-offs and ethical considerations. This not only sharpens participants' analytical skills but also encourages a collaborative, open approach to problem-solving.

How Case Studies Promote Decision-Making, Problem-Solving, and Collaborative Discussions

At their core, case studies are designed to promote decision-making and problem-solving by placing participants in realistic scenarios that mirror the challenges they will face in leadership roles. By actively engaging with the material, participants are forced to wrestle with difficult questions, test their leadership skills, and learn from both successes and mistakes.

1. Encouraging Structured Decision-Making

In the real world, decisions are rarely made in isolation. Leaders must weigh multiple factors, from financial impacts to stakeholder interests, while also considering long-term consequences. Case studies provide a platform for participants to practice structured decision-making by breaking down complex problems into manageable pieces.

Consider the example of Arclight Energy, a fictional utility company facing operational disruptions due to a natural disaster. As the CEO, participants must decide whether to allocate resources toward immediate repairs or invest in long-term infrastructure improvements to mitigate future risks. Each option has its trade-offs—repairing the current damage may be less costly, but failing to address underlying vulnerabilities could lead to larger issues down the road. By encouraging participants to evaluate these options carefully, the case study promotes structured, thoughtful decision-making.

2. Fostering Creative Problem-Solving

Many case studies present problems that require creative solutions. Often, the most obvious solution is not necessarily the best one, and participants must think outside the box to address the issue effectively. By fostering creativity, case studies help leaders develop innovative approaches to solving problems.

In the Arclight Energy scenario, one group of participants might propose partnering with the government to secure funding for infrastructure improvements, while another group suggests investing in renewable energy to diversify the company's assets. Both solutions involve creative problem-solving, as participants consider not only the immediate crisis but also how to position the company for long-term success.

3. Promoting Collaborative Discussions

Leadership is rarely a solo endeavor. Leaders must collaborate with teams, stakeholders, and other executives to make informed decisions. Case studies simulate this reality by encouraging participants to work together, discuss their ideas, and reach consensus.

For example, in a case study involving Terrabuild Construction, a fictional construction company, the management team is faced with a labor strike that threatens to delay a major project. The case study asks participants to collaborate as a management team, devising a strategy to address the workers' concerns while minimizing project disruptions. Some participants may propose increasing wages to resolve the strike quickly, while others might advocate for negotiating non-monetary benefits. Through these discussions, participants learn to navigate differing opinions and find a collaborative path forward.

In conclusion, case studies are an essential tool for leadership development because they mirror the complexities of real-world crises, forcing participants to engage in decision-making, problem-solving, and collaboration. When structured effectively, case studies challenge leaders to think critically, adapt to new information, and work together to find solutions. By using role-playing, real-time updates, and collaborative discussions, trainers can create an immersive learning environment where participants not only learn key leadership skills but also gain the confidence to apply those skills in their organizations. As such, case studies are not just training exercises—they are simulations that prepare leaders for the challenges of the real world.

Part 2:
Crisis Communication and Leadership in Action

Chapter 4: Crisis Communication Frameworks

Crisis communication is the backbone of leadership in moments of uncertainty and upheaval. In a crisis, the ability to deliver clear, timely, and accurate information can determine whether the organization emerges from the situation intact or suffers significant long-term damage. A well-structured communication strategy helps leaders keep stakeholders informed, calm employees, manage media narratives, and ultimately safeguard the organization's reputation.

This chapter will explore the importance of communication during crises, provide a comprehensive framework for engaging with different stakeholders, and offer a thought-provoking case study to illustrate these concepts in action.

The Importance of Clear Communication During a Crisis

In any crisis, uncertainty fuels fear, speculation, and misinformation. Without clear communication, employees may become confused about their roles, customers may lose confidence in the organization, and the media may fill the void with damaging speculation. Effective leaders understand that communication is not just about relaying facts—it's about guiding perception, setting expectations, and instilling confidence in those affected by the crisis.

Imagine Summit Innovations, a leading tech company, facing a sudden data breach that compromises the sensitive information of millions of users. The leadership team, headed by CEO John

Aldridge, is confronted with a chaotic situation. Employees are unsure of what to do, customers are panicking over their exposed data, and the media is relentlessly pursuing answers. In the absence of a clear communication strategy, the situation could spiral out of control. This example highlights the necessity of proactive communication in managing crises, demonstrating how leaders can either alleviate or exacerbate tensions based on their approach.

When handled poorly, lack of communication or inconsistent messaging can lead to disastrous consequences. For instance, an organization that withholds information from stakeholders may appear deceitful, while contradictory messages to employees may sow confusion and distrust. In contrast, when leaders are transparent and consistent in their messaging, they can maintain trust and control the narrative, even in the most challenging circumstances.

Framework for Communicating with Stakeholders, Employees, and Media

Successful crisis communication requires a structured framework that addresses the unique needs of different stakeholders. Each group—whether they are employees, customers, partners, investors, or the media—will have its own concerns and expectations. The framework must be designed to meet those needs while delivering a unified, coherent message.

1. Identifying Key Stakeholders

The first step in crisis communication is identifying the primary stakeholders who need to be addressed. These typically include:

- ✓ **Employees:** They are the organization's most important asset, and their confidence in leadership is crucial. Communication with employees should be clear, consistent, and supportive, ensuring they understand their roles during the crisis and feel reassured about the company's direction.
- ✓ **Customers and Clients:** Customer trust can erode quickly during a crisis, especially if they feel their needs are being ignored or their information is at risk. Communication with customers should be swift and empathetic, offering reassurance and practical steps to resolve any issues they are facing.
- ✓ **Investors and Business Partners:** Investors want to know how the crisis will impact the organization's financial health, while business partners may be concerned about disruptions in operations or supply chains. Keeping these groups informed helps preserve confidence in the organization's long-term viability.
- ✓ **Media and the Public:** The media plays a critical role in shaping public perception. Clear, timely communication with the media ensures that the organization's narrative is accurately represented and helps prevent rumors or misinformation from spreading.

2. Developing a Unified Message

A crisis often requires rapid response, but that doesn't mean communication should be rushed. The message delivered to stakeholders must be carefully crafted to ensure clarity, transparency, and consistency. It's important to address key questions such as:

- ✓ What has happened?

- ✓ What actions are being taken to resolve the crisis?
- ✓ How does the organization plan to prevent similar issues in the future?
- ✓ What are the immediate next steps for stakeholders?

Leaders must strike a balance between delivering factual updates and maintaining an empathetic tone. In a product recall scenario, for example, a company may need to admit fault, apologize to affected customers, and explain the steps being taken to rectify the issue—all without shifting blame or offering excuses.

3. Timing and Frequency of Communication

During a crisis, silence is not an option. The timing of communication is critical, and leaders must be proactive rather than reactive. Waiting too long to provide updates may create a perception of dishonesty or incompetence. Communication should occur at regular intervals to keep stakeholders informed of any new developments and to demonstrate that the leadership team is actively managing the situation.

For example, in a case where an airline faces a technical issue that grounds flights for hours, regular updates to passengers, even if the situation remains unresolved, can reduce frustration. Acknowledging that the company is working on a solution helps to maintain customer trust, even in the face of service disruption.

4. Engaging with the Media

When communicating with the media, it's essential to manage the narrative. The media will likely seek interviews, statements, or press releases to report on the crisis. Leaders must remain calm, factual, and composed during media engagements. Rather than deflecting blame or offering vague answers, they should focus on delivering the organization's side of the story with transparency.

Providing a clear statement and offering regular updates to media outlets can help prevent the spread of misinformation. For more complex situations, it's often wise to designate a specific spokesperson who can handle all media inquiries, ensuring a consistent message is delivered across all channels.

Case Study: Effective Communication During a Product Recall

Let's explore the case of Vista Nutrition, a successful health and wellness company that experienced a crisis when one of its top-selling nutritional supplements, VitaBoost, was found to contain potentially harmful contaminants. Thousands of customers had already purchased the product, and media outlets quickly picked up the story, creating a public outcry. Vista Nutrition faced the difficult task of managing the fallout and rebuilding trust with customers, investors, and the general public.

The Crisis Unfolds

Vista Nutrition's CEO, Claire Reynolds, was informed of the contamination issue when several customers reported adverse reactions after using VitaBoost. Internal tests confirmed the presence of a foreign substance in a batch of supplements, sparking an immediate recall. The company needed to act quickly, not only to prevent further harm to consumers but also to protect its reputation in the highly competitive wellness industry.

Step 1: Communicating with Employees

The first priority for Claire and her leadership team was to inform employees, especially those in customer-facing roles. Vista Nutrition held an emergency company-wide meeting to explain the situation, outline the steps being taken to address the issue, and provide clear instructions on how employees should handle customer inquiries.

During the meeting, Claire emphasized the importance of transparency, stating, "Our customers trust us with their health, and we owe it to them to be completely honest about what happened and what we're doing to fix it." Employees were provided with talking points and a FAQ document to ensure they had the information needed to support concerned customers.

Step 2: Engaging with Customers

Next, Vista Nutrition issued a public statement through multiple channels—social media, email, and the company's website. The message was clear and empathetic: "We deeply regret that a batch of VitaBoost supplements has been found to contain contaminants that could pose a health risk. If you have purchased this product, please stop using it immediately and return it for a full refund. We are investigating the cause of this issue and will provide updates as soon as possible."

The company also set up a dedicated hotline for customers to ask questions and receive support. By being upfront and providing clear instructions, Vista Nutrition sought to reassure its customers that the situation was under control.

Step 3: Engaging the Media

As media attention grew, Claire Reynolds agreed to a live interview with a major news network. Rather than dodging questions or deflecting blame, Claire took full responsibility for the crisis. “As CEO, I am accountable for everything that happens under my leadership, and I want to personally apologize to our customers for any harm this may have caused. We are committed to doing everything in our power to ensure this never happens again.”

Claire’s candid approach resonated with the public, and her willingness to face the media head-on helped Vista Nutrition regain some of the trust it had lost. The company continued to provide regular updates as the investigation into the contamination progressed, ensuring that both customers and the media were kept informed.

Step 4: Rebuilding Trust

In the months following the crisis, Vista Nutrition implemented stricter quality control measures, which were communicated to the public through a series of blog posts and press releases. The company also launched a customer loyalty program, offering discounts to those affected by the recall as a gesture of goodwill.

By maintaining open and honest communication throughout the crisis, Vista Nutrition was able to rebuild its reputation and reassure its stakeholders that it was committed to their safety and well-being.

In times of crisis, clear and effective communication is the difference between chaos and control. Leaders must adopt a structured communication framework that addresses the needs of all stakeholders, from employees to customers, investors, and the media. As demonstrated in the case of Vista Nutrition, timely and transparent communication can help mitigate damage, restore trust, and guide an organization through even the most challenging crises.

This chapter provides a roadmap for leaders to navigate the complexities of crisis communication, emphasizing the importance of consistency, empathy, and proactivity in managing both internal and external stakeholders. By mastering these communication strategies, leaders can turn potential disasters into opportunities for growth and demonstrate their ability to lead with confidence under pressure.

Chapter 5: Leadership Traits During Crisis

Crisis often serves as the ultimate test of leadership. In the midst of uncertainty, the actions and decisions of leaders have the power to either steer an organization toward stability or drive it further into chaos. The traits that distinguish great leaders in times of crisis are not merely technical skills but deeply rooted personal qualities that allow them to act with clarity, strength, and compassion. In this chapter, we explore three critical leadership traits that are essential in a crisis: decisiveness, empathy, and resilience. We'll also examine how these traits can be applied to lead with confidence under pressure, drawing on a case study of a CEO who successfully led his company through a reputation crisis.

Critical Leadership Traits Needed During Crises

Crises come in many forms—financial upheavals, operational failures, reputational damage, or even environmental disasters. Each scenario presents unique challenges, but the fundamental leadership traits that help navigate these storms remain the same. Leaders who demonstrate decisiveness, empathy, and resilience can inspire confidence, guide their teams, and make the tough calls necessary to move forward. These qualities are the bedrock of crisis leadership, allowing individuals to remain calm under pressure and make sound decisions in the face of uncertainty.

Decisiveness

During a crisis, information is often incomplete, and

the landscape is rapidly changing. A decisive leader can cut through the noise, make quick decisions based on the best available information, and pivot as new data emerges. Indecision, on the other hand, can paralyze an organization, creating a vacuum where uncertainty festers. Decisive leaders inspire confidence because they provide clear direction even when the path forward is uncertain.

Take the example of GlobalWave Industries, a manufacturing company that faced a sudden supply chain disruption when a key supplier unexpectedly went bankrupt. CEO Aaron Miller was forced to act quickly to secure alternative suppliers to keep production running. In less than 48 hours, Aaron mobilized his procurement team, negotiated with new partners, and made the decision to temporarily increase production costs to maintain delivery schedules. While some criticized the cost increase, Aaron's decisiveness prevented the company from missing crucial deadlines, ultimately preserving client relationships and protecting the company's reputation.

Empathy

While decisiveness is critical for making timely decisions, empathy is what ensures leaders stay connected to the human element of a crisis. A leader who can put themselves in the shoes of employees, customers, and stakeholders fosters trust and loyalty. Empathy enables leaders to communicate in a way that acknowledges the fears and concerns of others, showing that they care not just about business outcomes, but also about the well-being of those affected.

During the height of the COVID-19 pandemic, MapleHealth Solutions, a mid-sized healthcare company, faced a staffing crisis as many employees were forced to quarantine. CEO Elena Garza was confronted with tough choices—overworked staff, frightened patients, and rising demands on the healthcare system. Instead of focusing solely on operational metrics, Elena made it a priority to connect with employees personally. She held town hall meetings to hear their concerns, offered mental health resources, and implemented a flexible leave policy to help ease the burden. Elena's empathy not only helped maintain employee morale but also fostered a culture of trust that motivated her staff to go the extra mile for patients during a critical time.

Resilience

Crises often take a toll on both leaders and their organizations. The ability to bounce back from setbacks and maintain a long-term perspective is a hallmark of resilience. Resilient leaders understand that the path through a crisis is rarely linear; setbacks are inevitable, and the ability to adapt, learn from mistakes, and press forward is essential.

Consider Aurora Tech, a growing startup that experienced a major cyberattack that compromised client data. Founder and CEO Michael Barrett was initially overwhelmed by the magnitude of the breach and its potential impact on the company's future. But instead of succumbing to the pressure, Michael approached the crisis with a resilient mindset. He worked tirelessly with his IT and legal teams to assess the damage, notify affected clients, and implement enhanced security protocols. Throughout the ordeal, Michael maintained a calm and determined demeanor, reassuring employees and clients alike that Aurora Tech would emerge stronger. His resilience paid off—the company not only survived the crisis but gained new clients due to its transparency and improved security measures.

How to Lead with Confidence Under Pressure

Leading with confidence during a crisis does not mean pretending to have all the answers or being immune to doubt. Instead, it involves a willingness to act, communicate openly, and instill a sense of direction and hope. Leaders who can project confidence without arrogance inspire their teams to remain focused and proactive, even when the situation seems bleak.

1. Communicate Transparently

In times of crisis, uncertainty breeds fear. A confident leader knows that transparency—being open about what is known, what is unknown, and what is being done—helps alleviate anxiety. While it's tempting to withhold information until every detail is confirmed, delaying communication can erode trust. By sharing information as it becomes available, even if it's imperfect, leaders demonstrate confidence in their ability to manage the situation.

2. Empower Your Team

A confident leader understands that they cannot handle every aspect of the crisis alone. Empowering others to take ownership of specific tasks not only lightens the load but also creates a sense of collective responsibility. In doing so, leaders show trust in their teams' abilities, which in turn boosts morale and fosters a collaborative approach to problem-solving.

3. Stay Calm and Focused

One of the most noticeable qualities of confident leadership during a crisis is composure. When a leader remains calm under pressure, it sets the tone for the rest of the organization. Panic spreads quickly, but so does confidence. A leader's ability to stay focused on the larger picture, while managing the immediate details of the crisis, helps the entire team maintain perspective.

Case Study: Leading Through a Reputation Crisis

In 2018, Pioneer Apparel, a popular clothing brand known for its eco-friendly products, was thrust into a reputation crisis when a whistleblower accused the company of unethical labor practices at one of its overseas factories. The news spread rapidly through social media, tarnishing the brand's reputation as a champion of sustainability and ethical business practices. The CEO, Rachel Dawson, faced a public backlash, calls for boycotts, and media scrutiny. Pioneer Apparel's future was at risk, and Rachel had to lead the company through this storm.

Step 1: Decisive Action

Rachel immediately understood the severity of the allegations and recognized that any delay in response would only amplify the damage. Within 24 hours of the whistleblower's report going public, Rachel issued a public statement acknowledging the situation. She did not deny the allegations but promised a thorough investigation, reassuring stakeholders that the company would take corrective action if the claims were substantiated. Internally, she assembled a crisis team to assess the facts and determine the appropriate response.

Rachel's swift and decisive action set the tone for how the company would handle the crisis. By taking ownership from the outset, she signaled to customers, employees, and investors that Pioneer

Apparel was committed to transparency and accountability.

Step 2: Empathy and Transparency

Understanding the anger and disappointment of customers, Rachel made empathy a cornerstone of the company's crisis communication. In her public address, she expressed deep concern over the allegations, acknowledging how they undermined the trust that the company had worked hard to build. "As a leader, I am heartbroken to hear that we may have failed to uphold our values," Rachel said. "I want our customers to know that their concerns are valid, and we are fully committed to making things right."

Rachel did not hide behind corporate jargon or deflect responsibility. Her communication was direct, personal, and transparent. As the investigation continued, she provided regular updates to stakeholders, including details about the steps the company was taking to improve working conditions at its factories.

Step 3: Resilience and Long-Term Change

The investigation revealed several lapses in oversight at one of Pioneer Apparel's contracted factories, confirming some of the whistleblower's claims. Rather than trying to downplay the findings, Rachel took bold steps to implement lasting changes. The company terminated its contract with the factory, revamped its supply chain auditing process, and introduced a new code of ethics that required all suppliers to meet stringent labor standards.

Rachel's resilience was evident in her commitment to turning the crisis into an opportunity for growth. She did not view the scandal as a failure, but as a turning point for the company. Under her leadership, Pioneer Apparel not only recovered its reputation but also gained a new level of respect for its proactive measures. The company even received recognition from several environmental and labor organizations for its enhanced sustainability and ethics programs.

Conclusion

Leadership during a crisis is not about having all the answers or controlling every outcome. It's about demonstrating the core traits of decisiveness, empathy, and resilience to guide an organization through uncertainty. Leaders who act swiftly, communicate openly, and maintain their focus under pressure can steer their teams toward stability and even use the crisis as a catalyst for long-term positive change.

The case study of Pioneer Apparel illustrates how a CEO's ability to act decisively, communicate with empathy, and remain resilient in the face of a reputational crisis can not only save a company but strengthen its values and future direction. Leaders who master these traits are well-equipped to manage the complexities of any crisis, no matter the scale or intensity.

Chapter 6:
Crisis Decision-Making Frameworks

In times of crisis, decision-making becomes more than just an organizational necessity—it transforms into a matter of survival. Every choice made during such periods can have lasting consequences for the company's reputation, financial health, and even its very existence. Decisions must often be made quickly, under significant pressure, and with incomplete information. In this chapter, we explore structured approaches to decision-making during uncertainty, tools and frameworks that can help assess risks and options, and a detailed case study of how a board of directors successfully navigated a financial meltdown.

Structured Approaches to Decision-Making in Times of Uncertainty

Crises by nature introduce unpredictability. Information can be scarce or unreliable, emotions run high, and the stakes are elevated. To manage these dynamics, leaders must rely on structured decision-making frameworks that provide a clear path forward. These frameworks allow leaders to make well-considered choices even when time is of the essence. A strong framework guides leaders through evaluating the severity of the crisis, understanding potential consequences, and identifying the best course of action.

One such approach is the **OODA Loop**, which stands for Observe, Orient, Decide, and Act. Originally developed for military strategy, the OODA

Loop is a rapid decision-making process that enables leaders to adapt quickly to changing circumstances:

- ✓ **Observe**: Collect relevant information about the crisis. What are the immediate facts? What is happening within the organization, and what external factors are influencing the crisis?
- ✓ **Orient**: Interpret the information by assessing the internal and external environments. How does this situation compare to past crises? What are the key drivers, and how are different stakeholders affected?
- ✓ **Decide**: Based on the interpretation of the data, decide on a course of action. Multiple options should be considered, and the chosen path should balance risks and opportunities.
- ✓ **Act**: Implement the decision promptly, with a focus on flexibility. Since crises are fluid, the response may need to adapt as the situation evolves.

Another structured approach is the **DECIDE model**, commonly used in aviation but highly relevant for business crises:

- ✓ **D**efine the problem.
- ✓ **E**stablish criteria for success.
- ✓ **C**onsider all possible options.
- ✓ **I**dentify the best option.
- ✓ **D**evelop a plan to implement the decision.
- ✓ **E**valuate the outcome to ensure objectives are met.

Both frameworks allow leaders to move through decision-making processes methodically, ensuring that action is taken without delay but with sufficient rigor to avoid impulsive mistakes. These methods are especially useful for managing high-stakes, complex crises, where it is critical to keep a clear head while simultaneously moving fast.

Tools and Frameworks to Assess Options and Risks During Crises

In addition to structured decision-making processes, leaders benefit from using specific tools and frameworks that allow them to assess options and measure risk in real time. Such tools give decision-makers the ability to weigh potential actions against their associated risks and rewards, ensuring that decisions are both strategic and sound.

1. Risk Matrix

A simple but effective tool for evaluating risk is the Risk Matrix, which helps leaders visually plot potential outcomes based on two criteria: the likelihood of the event occurring and the severity of its impact. The matrix is divided into quadrants ranging from low likelihood/low impact to high likelihood/high impact. This tool allows leaders to prioritize responses, focusing on the most critical risks first. During crises, the matrix helps leaders avoid being overwhelmed by the sheer volume of potential threats by directing attention to those that are most urgent.

For instance, in the case of a potential supply chain breakdown, the likelihood of disruption might be moderate, but the impact could be severe, placing the issue in the "high risk" quadrant and demanding immediate attention.

2. SWOT Analysis

While often associated with strategic planning, the SWOT analysis (Strengths, Weaknesses, Opportunities, Threats) can be a valuable tool during crises as well. It encourages leaders to evaluate not just the risks but also the resources and opportunities that may emerge from the crisis. Identifying internal strengths (such as a strong, loyal customer base) can help leaders leverage these assets, while acknowledging weaknesses (such as outdated IT infrastructure) informs risk mitigation efforts.

3. Decision Trees

Decision Trees provide a visual way to map out the various courses of action available during a crisis and predict the potential outcomes of each. Each "branch" represents a decision point, with subsequent branches splitting into further decisions and outcomes. This tool is especially useful when navigating complex crises with multiple layers of uncertainty. Decision trees help leaders visualize the impact of each decision and make informed choices based on potential consequences.

For example, a company facing a legal dispute might map out its options: settle the case, fight in court, or negotiate a compromise. Each of these options leads to different outcomes, and by weighing the risks and benefits of each, leaders can make a more informed decision about the path forward.

Case Study: Navigating a Financial Meltdown

In 2020, Harper-Morgan Holdings, a private equity firm specializing in real estate investments, faced an existential crisis when the global pandemic caused sudden disruptions in the real estate market. Many of their portfolio companies—comprising hotels, commercial properties, and retail outlets—were suddenly unable to meet their financial obligations. Rent collections plummeted, vacancies soared, and investor confidence hit an all-time low. As the markets spiraled, the company's liquidity dried up, putting them at risk of bankruptcy.

Step 1: Observing the Situation

The board of Harper-Morgan immediately convened a crisis meeting to assess the situation. Using the OODA Loop as their framework, they gathered data on their financial position. The key issue was clear: without immediate cash flow, the firm would be unable to service its debts, and its investors would lose millions. Additionally, they faced reputational risk if they had to close several properties in highly visible locations.

Step 2: Orienting

Next, the board oriented themselves by looking at the external factors driving the crisis. The pandemic had created an unprecedented demand drop across all of their portfolio sectors. However, they noticed that residential properties in certain areas were still doing well due to people relocating to smaller cities to escape urban density. This insight helped the board identify one area of relative strength amidst the devastation.

Step 3: Deciding on a Course of Action

The board then used a Decision Tree framework to map out their options. The first decision was whether to try to sell off assets quickly to raise liquidity or hold onto the properties in hopes of a market recovery. Selling assets under distress would bring in much-needed cash but risked deep losses. Holding the assets might stave off short-term disaster but could lead to a deeper crisis if the market didn't recover fast enough.

Using a combination of the Risk Matrix and SWOT analysis, the board assessed the likelihood of market recovery and their internal strengths. While they had liquidity problems, they also had strong relationships with their financial backers and a reputation for sound investments. They decided on a hybrid approach: sell off the least profitable properties quickly to secure some liquidity but hold onto the prime assets that had the potential for long-term gains.

Step 4: Taking Action

Once the decision was made, the firm acted swiftly. They contacted buyers for their non-core assets, renegotiated loan terms with lenders, and communicated openly with investors about the steps they were taking to navigate the crisis. At the same time, they reached out to local governments to participate in relief programs that allowed them to defer certain payments and minimize losses.

Step 5: Evaluating the Outcome

Over the next several months, Harper-Morgan weathered the storm. The firm successfully sold off several properties, raising enough capital to meet their short-term obligations. As the pandemic eased, their decision to hold onto key properties paid off, with the real estate market rebounding faster than anticipated. Their transparency with investors and decisive actions also earned them respect in the financial community, enhancing their reputation even in the midst of adversity.

Crises require leaders to make decisions in environments of heightened uncertainty, where both time and information are limited. By employing structured decision-making frameworks such as the OODA Loop, the DECIDE model, and tools like Risk Matrices, SWOT analysis, and Decision Trees, leaders can navigate these turbulent periods with greater confidence and clarity. These frameworks allow leaders to systematically assess risks, consider various options, and make informed decisions, even when the stakes are high.

The case study of Harper-Morgan Holdings demonstrates how a board can use these tools to manage a financial meltdown. Their approach—combining quick action with strategic thinking and transparency—allowed the company not only to survive the crisis but also to position itself for long-term success. Leaders who master these frameworks will be better equipped to guide their organizations through even the most complex and challenging crises.

Part 3:
Managing Financial Crises

Chapter 7:
Financial Crises in Corporations

Financial crises can strike even the most well-established corporations, threatening their survival and reputation. These crises typically arise from a combination of factors, including liquidity issues, market crashes, and poor investments. When managed improperly, they can lead to the collapse of businesses that were once thriving. However, with the right leadership, even companies on the brink of disaster can recover and emerge stronger than before. In this chapter, we will examine the common causes of financial crises, explore how leaders can mitigate financial risks, and delve into a real-life case study of a company that successfully recovered from near bankruptcy.

Common Causes of Financial Crises

While financial crises are unique to each company and situation, there are several common causes that often play a critical role in their development. Understanding these causes is crucial for leaders who want to anticipate and mitigate risks before they escalate into full-blown crises.

1. Liquidity Issues

Liquidity is the lifeblood of any business, and when a company is unable to meet its short-term obligations—such as paying employees, suppliers, or creditors—it faces immediate operational challenges. Liquidity issues often arise when there is a mismatch between cash inflows and outflows. Even profitable companies can fall into a liquidity crisis if their assets are tied up in investments or inventory that cannot be converted to cash quickly enough to meet immediate financial obligations. When a company runs out of cash, it can quickly spiral into insolvency, triggering layoffs, missed payments, and a loss of confidence from investors and stakeholders.

2. Market Crashes

External market forces, such as stock market crashes or sudden economic downturns, can have a devastating impact on corporate finances. Companies that are overly dependent on a specific market or economic condition are especially vulnerable when that market collapses. For instance, companies tied to the housing market in 2008 found themselves in a precarious position when the housing bubble burst, leading to widespread financial ruin. Such market crashes not only decrease the value of assets and investments but also reduce consumer confidence, leading to lower sales, tighter credit, and reduced liquidity.

3. Poor Investments and Strategic Missteps

In some cases, financial crises are the result of poor investment decisions or misguided strategies. Leaders who pursue overly aggressive expansion plans, invest in high-risk ventures, or fail to adapt to changing market conditions can put their companies in jeopardy. For example, investing in a declining industry or entering a new market without adequate research and preparation can lead to substantial losses. When combined with other financial pressures, these poor investment choices can create a perfect storm that drives the company toward bankruptcy.

How Leaders Can Mitigate Financial Risks

Effective leadership is essential in both preventing financial crises and navigating through them when they occur. Leaders who are proactive in managing risks can protect their organizations from the worst effects of a financial meltdown and, in some cases, even turn a crisis into an opportunity for growth.

1. Maintaining Strong Liquidity Buffers

One of the most important steps leaders can take to mitigate financial risks is ensuring the company maintains a strong liquidity buffer. This means keeping enough cash or easily accessible assets on hand to cover short-term obligations, even in the event of an unexpected downturn. Companies with robust liquidity positions are far better equipped to weather crises without resorting to desperate measures, such as selling valuable assets at a loss or taking on unsustainable levels of debt. Leaders should regularly assess their company's liquidity position and create contingency plans for addressing any potential shortfalls.

2. Diversifying Revenue Streams

Leaders should also focus on diversifying their company's revenue streams to reduce dependency on any one market, product, or customer base. By spreading risks across multiple income sources, companies can better withstand market fluctuations. For example, a company that relies exclusively on sales from a single product line is highly vulnerable if demand for that product drops unexpectedly. Diversifying revenue sources by investing in new markets or expanding the product portfolio can reduce this risk and ensure greater financial stability.

3. Regularly Assessing Investment Risks

Before making major investments or strategic moves, leaders must conduct thorough due diligence to assess potential risks and rewards. This involves analyzing market trends, competitive landscapes, and the long-term viability of the investment. Leaders should avoid taking on excessive debt to fund high-risk ventures and ensure that any new investment aligns with the company's overall strategic goals. In times of uncertainty, it is especially important for leaders to adopt a cautious and measured approach to investments.

4. Transparent Communication with Stakeholders

During financial crises, leaders must communicate openly and honestly with stakeholders, including employees, investors, and creditors. Transparency helps maintain trust, which is essential for securing the support needed to navigate through the crisis. Leaders who try to hide or downplay financial difficulties often lose credibility, which can exacerbate the crisis by triggering panic among stakeholders. Instead, effective leaders provide clear explanations of the challenges the company is facing and outline the steps they are taking to address them.

Case Study: The Recovery of Atlas Manufacturing

In 2017, Atlas Manufacturing, a mid-sized industrial equipment company, faced a financial crisis that brought it to the brink of bankruptcy. Founded in the early 1990s, Atlas had enjoyed steady growth for nearly two decades, supplying heavy machinery to construction and mining companies around the world. However, a series of poor investment decisions, combined with a sudden downturn in the global mining industry, pushed the company into a severe liquidity crisis.

The Roots of the Crisis

The crisis at Atlas began when its leadership team made a high-stakes decision to invest in a new line of cutting-edge drilling equipment. The company believed that this equipment would revolutionize the mining industry, giving it a significant competitive edge. To finance this investment, Atlas took on a large amount of debt, betting on the success of its new product. Unfortunately, the timing of the investment could not have been worse. Just as the new equipment was being launched, the global mining industry went into a deep recession, and demand for new machinery plummeted.

Atlas was left with massive inventory, substantial debt, and no way to generate the sales needed to cover its obligations. Within months, the company found itself unable to make payroll or meet its debt payments. Employees began to panic, and suppliers started demanding cash upfront for any new orders. Atlas was on the verge of declaring bankruptcy, with no clear path forward.

Leadership's Response

In the face of this crisis, Atlas's CEO, Martin Voss, knew he had to take decisive action to prevent the company from collapsing. Using a combination of the DECIDE model and financial restructuring strategies, Voss and his leadership team crafted a recovery plan aimed at stabilizing the company's finances and restoring stakeholder confidence.

The first step was to address the immediate liquidity crisis. Voss negotiated with Atlas's creditors to restructure the company's debt, securing a temporary moratorium on payments while the company worked to turn things around. At the same time, he initiated a series of cost-cutting measures, including layoffs and pay cuts, to reduce the company's operating expenses.

Recognizing the importance of transparency, Voss communicated openly with employees about the severity of the crisis and the steps the company was taking to recover. He held regular town hall meetings where employees could ask questions and voice concerns. This transparency helped ease some of the fear and uncertainty that had been spreading throughout the organization.

Turning the Crisis into an Opportunity

Next, Voss focused on diversifying Atlas's revenue streams. Rather than continuing to rely solely on the mining industry, he shifted the company's focus toward the renewable energy sector, which was experiencing rapid growth. Atlas adapted its machinery to serve the needs of wind and solar power companies, opening up new markets and revenue sources.

In parallel, Voss worked with a team of financial advisors to identify underperforming assets that could be sold to raise cash. The company sold off non-core business units and unused real estate, generating enough liquidity to keep operations running while it sought to rebuild its reputation and regain profitability.

The Outcome

Thanks to Voss's decisive leadership and the implementation of a clear recovery plan, Atlas Manufacturing managed to pull itself back from the brink of bankruptcy. Within two years, the company had returned to profitability, with diversified revenue streams and a leaner, more efficient operation. While the recovery process was painful—many employees lost their jobs, and some investors took significant losses—the company ultimately emerged stronger and more resilient.

Atlas's story demonstrates how effective leadership, transparent communication, and strategic decision-making can help a company recover from even the most dire financial crises. By taking swift action to address liquidity issues, diversifying revenue streams, and maintaining the trust of employees and stakeholders, leaders can guide their organizations through financial challenges and set them on a path to long-term success.

Financial crises are inevitable in the life of a corporation, but with the right leadership, they can be managed and even overcome. Whether caused by liquidity issues, market crashes, or poor investments, financial crises require decisive action and a clear plan for recovery. Leaders who understand the common causes of financial crises and take proactive steps to mitigate risks can prevent small problems from becoming catastrophic. The case of Atlas Manufacturing illustrates that even companies facing near bankruptcy can recover if they adopt a disciplined approach to decision-making, maintain transparency with stakeholders, and diversify their revenue streams. Leaders who master these skills will be well-equipped to navigate the complexities of managing financial crises and emerge stronger on the other side.

Chapter 8: Crisis Scenario Planning for Financial Survival

Financial crises can strike suddenly, often without warning. In these moments, businesses are forced to react under pressure, making decisions that can determine their very survival. However, organizations that proactively engage in crisis scenario planning have a significant advantage. By anticipating potential financial downturns and developing robust strategies to respond quickly, companies can mitigate the impact of crises and even turn challenges into opportunities for growth.

In this chapter, we explore the tools and frameworks that businesses can use to engage in scenario planning for financial crises. We will examine how leaders can prepare for worst-case scenarios and implement strategies for quick financial recovery. To illustrate the importance of scenario planning, we will also present a real-life case study of how a mid-sized manufacturing company avoided financial collapse by using scenario planning to anticipate and respond to a severe market disruption.

What is Scenario Planning?

Scenario planning is a strategic tool that enables organizations to envision and prepare for various future scenarios, especially those involving financial crises. Rather than focusing solely on the most likely outcome, scenario planning encourages businesses to consider multiple possibilities, including worst-case and best-case scenarios. By preparing for a range of potential crises, companies are better equipped to respond swiftly and effectively when unexpected events occur.

The core purpose of scenario planning is not to predict the future but to prepare for it. This proactive approach helps leaders identify early warning signs of a financial downturn, assess the potential impact on their organization, and devise contingency plans that can be activated as soon as a crisis emerges. Ultimately, scenario planning gives companies the flexibility to pivot quickly when circumstances change, reducing the likelihood of financial ruin.

Key Tools for Anticipating and Preparing for Financial Crises

To engage in effective scenario planning, businesses can utilize several tools and frameworks. These tools help organizations visualize potential crises, assess their financial vulnerability, and develop strategies for survival.

1. PESTLE Analysis

The PESTLE framework is an analytical tool that helps companies identify external factors that could influence their financial stability. PESTLE stands for Political, Economic, Social, Technological, Legal, and Environmental factors. By analyzing each of these areas, businesses can anticipate potential disruptions and incorporate them into their scenario planning.

For example, an economic downturn (Economic factor) or new government regulations (Political factor) could trigger a financial crisis for certain businesses. By examining the external environment through a PESTLE lens, leaders can better understand the potential threats and opportunities that might arise in the future.

2. Financial Stress Testing

Financial stress testing is a quantitative tool that allows companies to simulate how their financial performance might be affected under different stress scenarios. For example, a company might test how it would fare if revenue dropped by 25%, or if its supply chain was disrupted for six months. This helps leaders understand their financial resilience and highlights areas of vulnerability that need to be addressed.

Stress testing can be particularly valuable for assessing liquidity and debt management. Companies that discover they would run out of cash under a stress scenario can take preemptive action, such as building up cash reserves or renegotiating debt terms, to ensure they can weather a financial storm.

3. SWOT Analysis

SWOT analysis (Strengths, Weaknesses, Opportunities, Threats) is a widely used strategic tool that can help businesses evaluate their internal strengths and weaknesses while considering external opportunities and threats. In the context of scenario planning, SWOT analysis allows organizations to identify areas where they are most vulnerable to financial crises and develop strategies to mitigate those risks.

For example, a company might recognize that its heavy reliance on a single supplier (Weakness) exposes it to risk in the event of supply chain disruptions (Threat). By diversifying its supplier base (Opportunity), the company can reduce its financial exposure to potential crises.

Strategies for Quick Financial Recovery

Even with the best scenario planning, crises can still catch organizations off-guard. When financial trouble strikes, leaders must act quickly and decisively to stabilize the business and set it on a path to recovery. Here are some key strategies for recovering quickly from a financial crisis:

1. Prioritize Cash Flow

In any financial crisis, cash flow management is critical. Without sufficient cash on hand, businesses will struggle to meet their obligations, such as paying employees, suppliers, and creditors. During a crisis, leaders should prioritize cash flow above all else. This may involve cutting non-essential expenses, negotiating payment terms with creditors, or accelerating receivables. The goal is to ensure the company has enough liquidity to continue operating, even in the face of reduced revenue or increased costs.

2. Renegotiate Debt and Payment Terms

Companies that are burdened by high levels of debt can quickly find themselves in financial distress during a crisis. Leaders should engage in proactive negotiations with creditors to secure more favorable payment terms, such as extended deadlines or reduced interest rates. By renegotiating debt terms, businesses can alleviate some of the immediate financial pressure and free up cash to focus on recovery efforts.

3. Communicate Transparently with Stakeholders

Clear and transparent communication with stakeholders—employees, investors, suppliers, and customers—is essential during a financial crisis. When a company is facing financial trouble, rumors and uncertainty can spread quickly, leading to panic and loss of confidence. Leaders should provide regular updates on the company's financial position and recovery plan, reassuring stakeholders that they are taking decisive action to navigate the crisis. Transparency fosters trust and helps retain key stakeholders, which is crucial for long-term recovery.

4. Diversify Revenue Streams

One of the most effective ways to recover from a financial crisis is by diversifying revenue streams. Companies that are overly dependent on a single market, product, or customer base are more vulnerable during economic downturns. By expanding into new markets or developing new products, businesses can reduce their financial exposure and create new opportunities for growth. Diversification helps companies build resilience and recover more quickly from crises.

Case Study: Scenario Planning Saves GreenTech Industries

In 2018, GreenTech Industries, a renewable energy company specializing in solar panel manufacturing, was riding a wave of success. Demand for clean energy was at an all-time high, and GreenTech had secured lucrative contracts with several large utility companies. However, the company's leadership was aware of the volatile nature of the renewable energy market and had experienced firsthand the rapid shifts in government policies and market conditions that could occur in the industry. In anticipation of potential future challenges, GreenTech's CEO, Martha Nguyen, insisted on implementing a rigorous scenario planning process to prepare for any unforeseen crises.

The Scenario Planning Process

Under Nguyen's leadership, GreenTech engaged in scenario planning every six months, analyzing potential threats and opportunities that could impact the company's financial stability. One of the scenarios the company considered was a sudden reduction in government subsidies for solar energy—a critical factor driving demand for their products. While the company was experiencing high growth at the time, Nguyen knew that relying on government incentives made GreenTech vulnerable to policy changes.

Using a combination of PESTLE analysis and financial stress testing, GreenTech's leadership team simulated how the company would fare if subsidies were slashed by 50%. The results were sobering: the company's revenue would drop by 40% almost immediately, pushing it into a liquidity crisis within six months. Armed with this knowledge, Nguyen and her team developed a contingency plan to reduce the company's dependency on subsidies.

Implementation of the Contingency Plan

GreenTech's contingency plan included three key components. First, the company began diversifying its revenue streams by expanding into international markets where solar subsidies were less volatile. They focused on regions such as Southeast Asia and Africa, where demand for affordable, off-grid solar energy was growing rapidly.

Second, GreenTech invested in research and development to create more cost-effective solar panels. By lowering production costs, the company could remain competitive even in markets with reduced government incentives.

Finally, GreenTech built up its cash reserves, ensuring it had enough liquidity to weather a potential downturn. The company implemented cost-saving measures across all departments, freeing up cash that could be used to sustain operations during a crisis.

The Crisis Hits

In 2020, GreenTech's worst-case scenario became a reality. A change in political leadership in the company's home country led to a dramatic reduction in solar subsidies. Almost overnight, GreenTech's domestic sales plummeted by 35%. Several competitors that had not engaged in scenario planning were forced to shut down within months.

However, thanks to its proactive scenario planning, GreenTech was well-prepared. The company's international expansion efforts paid off, as new sales in Southeast Asia and Africa offset some of the losses in its domestic market. Meanwhile, the cost-cutting measures implemented through its R&D efforts allowed GreenTech to maintain profitability even with reduced revenue.

The Outcome

By the end of 2021, GreenTech had fully recovered from the crisis and was growing once again. While the solar industry as a whole experienced significant disruption, GreenTech's diversified revenue streams and leaner cost structure positioned it as one of the few survivors in a turbulent market. The company's experience with scenario planning not only saved it from financial collapse but also taught its leadership the value of anticipating and preparing for the unexpected.

Scenario planning is an essential tool for anticipating and preparing for financial crises. By exploring a range of potential scenarios and developing contingency plans, businesses can avoid being caught off-guard when a crisis strikes. The story of GreenTech Industries demonstrates how effective scenario planning can save a company from financial collapse, allowing it to recover quickly and continue to thrive.

Leaders who invest in scenario planning are better equipped to identify vulnerabilities, assess risks, and develop strategies for quick recovery. In times of uncertainty, this proactive approach can make the difference between survival and failure. As we have seen in this chapter, the ability to envision and prepare for future crises is a key leadership trait that sets successful companies apart from those that succumb to financial difficulties.

Part 4:
Managing Reputational Crises

Chapter 9: The Impact of Reputation on Business

In today's interconnected world, a company's reputation is often one of its most valuable assets. A positive reputation fosters trust among customers, investors, and the general public, creating a foundation for long-term success. Conversely, reputational damage can erode that trust, leading to lost revenue, legal challenges, and even business collapse. This chapter will explore the critical role that reputation plays in determining a company's success or failure. We will examine common reputational risks, such as scandals, legal battles, and public relations issues, and detail how proactive management can mitigate the impact of these crises. Finally, a case study will illustrate how a CEO successfully restored a company's image after a major public relations disaster.

Why Reputation is Crucial for Success and Survival

A strong reputation is the bedrock of business success. It acts as a silent ambassador, influencing how stakeholders perceive a company's values, integrity, and reliability. In many cases, customers choose a brand not just for its products or services but for what the brand stands for. Whether it's a commitment to quality, environmental responsibility, or social justice, a positive reputation sets businesses apart in a competitive market.

However, reputation is a double-edged sword—while it takes years to build, it can be damaged in an instant. In the age of social media, where news spreads rapidly, even a small incident can escalate into a full-blown crisis. Once trust is eroded, rebuilding it is an uphill battle that requires significant time, resources, and effort.

Consider companies like CleanPure Water (a fictitious example), which is known for its high-quality, environmentally sustainable bottled water. Over years, it built a solid reputation by emphasizing its environmental commitments. This reputation allowed CleanPure to charge premium prices and dominate its market. Its reputation became its most important asset, with customers associating the brand with clean, eco-friendly living.

When reputational crises strike, the impact is felt across every facet of a business—sales plummet, partnerships dissolve, and employee morale declines. Worse, a company's tarnished reputation can cause long-term harm, affecting investor confidence and customer loyalty for years to come. That's why managing reputation is not just a public relations effort—it is a business imperative.

Common Reputational Risks

The nature of reputational crises can vary, but they often arise from three common sources: scandals, legal battles, and public relations issues. Each of these threats, if not handled properly, can quickly escalate and lead to significant damage.

1. Scandals

Scandals, whether related to unethical behavior, fraud, or personal misconduct, are a primary cause of reputational damage. When companies or their leaders engage in unethical activities, they betray the trust of their stakeholders. In such cases, the damage can be long-lasting and difficult to repair, especially if the company is slow to respond or fails to acknowledge its wrongdoing.

For example, a pharmaceutical company might face a scandal over price gouging, leading to public outrage and a drop in stock value. Even if the company is legally within its rights, the perception of greed or exploitation can permanently harm its reputation.

2. Legal Battles

Legal battles, especially high-profile lawsuits, can cast a shadow over a company's image. Whether the case involves product liability, environmental violations, or employee disputes, the publicity surrounding a lawsuit can lead to reputational damage, even before a verdict is reached. The legal implications may result in financial losses, but the reputational consequences can be much more damaging in the long run.

Imagine a company like Greenfield Grocers, an organic food retailer (fictitious), being sued for mislabeling non-organic products as organic. Even if the company wins the lawsuit, the public might continue to view it with skepticism, questioning the integrity of its products and marketing practices.

3. Public Relations Issues

Public relations issues often arise from poor communication or missteps in handling a sensitive situation. In the age of social media, PR crises can spread quickly, fueled by misinformation or public outrage. A poorly worded statement or an ill-conceived advertisement can go viral for the wrong reasons, tarnishing a company's brand image. The real challenge lies in responding swiftly and appropriately to contain the damage.

Consider the case of NewSky Airlines, a budget airline known for its affordability and convenience. When a video of a passenger being forcibly removed from an overbooked flight went viral, the company initially responded with a dismissive statement that only exacerbated public anger. This poor handling of the situation caused widespread boycotts and a significant drop in bookings.

Strategies for Managing Reputational Crises

Managing a reputational crisis requires a delicate balance between immediate action and long-term planning. The key is to respond quickly and transparently while focusing on rebuilding trust over time.

1. Acknowledge the Problem

The first and most crucial step in managing a reputational crisis is to acknowledge the problem. Trying to cover up or downplay the issue only fuels public distrust. Instead, companies must take responsibility for their actions and demonstrate a willingness to make things right. Even in cases where the company is not at fault, an empathetic response can go a long way in calming public outrage.

2. Communicate Transparently

In any crisis, communication is key. Companies must provide clear, honest, and timely updates to all stakeholders, including employees, customers, and the media. This transparency reassures the public that the company is taking the crisis seriously and working to resolve the issue.

3. Take Corrective Action

Once the crisis is acknowledged, the company must take concrete steps to address the underlying issue. This might involve launching an internal investigation, terminating unethical employees, or implementing new policies to prevent future problems. The goal is to demonstrate that the company is committed to learning from its mistakes and taking corrective action.

4. Focus on Rebuilding Trust

Rebuilding trust after a reputational crisis is a long-term process. It requires consistent effort to restore the company's image, both through improved business practices and continued transparent communication. Companies that can show they have learned from their mistakes and are making meaningful changes are more likely to regain public trust over time.

Case Study: Restoring the Reputation of SilverLine Finance

In 2017, SilverLine Finance, a mid-sized financial services company, was riding high on its reputation for ethical business practices and customer-centric policies. Founded by John Wallace, a charismatic CEO with a passion for responsible investing, the company had gained a loyal customer base by promoting transparency and offering financial products tailored to individual needs. Wallace's leadership had positioned SilverLine as a beacon of trust in an industry often criticized for predatory practices.

However, SilverLine's reputation was severely tested when a former employee accused the company of falsifying records related to customer accounts. The employee, David Harris, claimed that the company had manipulated client portfolios to inflate profits and deceive investors. When Harris's allegations were made public, they quickly garnered media attention, sparking outrage among SilverLine's clients and shareholders. The company's stock price plummeted, and customers began withdrawing their investments in droves.

The Crisis Unfolds

In the immediate aftermath of the accusations, SilverLine's leadership was caught off guard. While the company vehemently denied Harris's claims, the damage had already been done. The public perception of the company had shifted overnight from that of a trusted financial institution to one embroiled in a potentially explosive scandal. SilverLine's initial response—issuing a brief statement dismissing Harris's allegations as baseless—only fueled the growing mistrust. Clients felt that the company was being evasive and dismissive of their concerns.

As the crisis deepened, Wallace realized that SilverLine needed a more comprehensive and transparent approach to restore its reputation. He convened an emergency board meeting and, after lengthy discussions with legal and public relations experts, decided to take a bold step: he would personally address the allegations in a live press conference and announce a full, independent investigation into the company's practices.

The Path to Redemption

During the press conference, Wallace took full responsibility for the company's failure to address the allegations earlier. He emphasized that SilverLine had nothing to hide and was fully committed to transparency. Wallace announced that the company had hired an independent third-party audit firm to conduct a thorough investigation into its financial records and client portfolios. He also pledged to share the audit's findings with the public, regardless of the outcome.

Wallace's candid and proactive approach had an immediate impact. While some clients remained skeptical, many appreciated his willingness to confront the issue head-on. The independent investigation took several months, but when the results were finally released, they vindicated SilverLine. The audit found no evidence of wrongdoing and confirmed that the company's financial practices were sound.

Armed with the audit results, Wallace embarked on a comprehensive campaign to rebuild SilverLine's reputation. He met personally with major clients, addressed employee concerns in town hall meetings, and worked closely with the company's PR team to ensure that the public understood the findings. Over the next year, SilverLine launched new initiatives to improve transparency, including offering clients more detailed reports on their investments and implementing stricter internal controls to prevent future issues.

The Outcome

By 2019, SilverLine had regained much of the trust it had lost. While some clients had left the company for good, many returned after seeing the results of the audit and witnessing Wallace's commitment to reform. The company's stock price stabilized, and new clients were drawn to SilverLine's reputation for transparency and ethical business practices.

The experience taught Wallace and his team the importance of proactive communication and transparency in managing a reputational crisis.

SilverLine's swift recovery from a potentially catastrophic scandal demonstrated that businesses can overcome even the most serious reputational challenges if they are willing to take responsibility, communicate openly, and implement meaningful changes.

Reputation is one of the most valuable assets a company can have, but it is also one of the most fragile. Businesses must be vigilant in safeguarding their reputation and prepared to act quickly when crises arise. As the case of SilverLine Finance illustrates, managing a reputational crisis requires not only addressing the immediate problem but also committing to long-term reforms that restore public trust. In the end, reputation is not just about how a company is perceived today but how it is remembered in the future.

Chapter 10:
Restoring Reputation After a Crisis

A crisis can strike any organization at any time, and when it does, the company's reputation is often one of the first casualties. The digital age has amplified this risk, as social media and 24-hour news cycles make it easier than ever for negative information to spread rapidly. In many cases, a single incident can undo years of hard work and positive branding, leading to a widespread loss of trust among customers, investors, and employees. Restoring reputation after a crisis requires a well-thought-out and strategic approach that balances immediate damage control with long-term rebuilding of trust.

In this chapter, we will explore effective crisis response strategies that can help companies manage the media, navigate public perception, and protect their brand reputation. We will also outline the key steps to rebuilding trust with stakeholders after the dust settles. Finally, we will present a case study of a global brand that successfully overcame a significant reputational crisis, demonstrating that recovery is possible with the right approach.

Crisis Response Strategies: Managing the Media, Public Perception, and Brand Reputation

The first step in restoring reputation after a crisis is managing the immediate fallout. This typically involves controlling the narrative and preventing misinformation from spiraling out of control. When a company faces a crisis—whether it's a product recall, executive misconduct, or a public scandal—how it responds in the early stages can make or break its recovery efforts.

1. Acknowledge the Crisis Early

One of the biggest mistakes companies make is delaying their response. When a crisis hits, the worst thing a company can do is stay silent or offer vague statements. The public and the media want answers, and a lack of information can lead to speculation, rumors, and distrust. An early acknowledgment, even if it's just to say the company is aware of the situation and is investigating, can buy valuable time and help reassure the public that the company is taking the matter seriously.

For instance, when GlobalTech Solutions, a large electronics manufacturer, discovered that one of its flagship products was causing malfunctions in customer devices, they immediately issued a press statement acknowledging the issue and assuring customers that they were working on a solution. By addressing the problem early on, they avoided accusations of covering up the defect and maintained a level of transparency that helped mitigate the initial damage.

2. Control the Narrative

Once a company has acknowledged the crisis, it is critical to take control of the narrative. This means proactively communicating with the media and the public, rather than allowing others to shape the story. A crisis management team should be in place to handle press inquiries, monitor social media, and ensure that the company's side of the story is heard.

Crafting clear, consistent messages across all channels—press releases, social media, and internal communications—is essential. During a crisis, mixed messaging can confuse stakeholders and further erode trust. It's important to provide regular updates, even if the investigation is ongoing, so that stakeholders feel informed and reassured.

When ClearAir Industries, a company specializing in air purification systems, faced accusations that its products were emitting harmful chemicals, the company quickly mobilized a media team to address the claims. They released a detailed report on the safety of their products, held press conferences, and engaged with customers on social media to address concerns. This proactive approach allowed them to control the narrative and prevent the situation from escalating further.

3. Take Responsibility Where Necessary

In some cases, the company may need to take full responsibility for the crisis. Whether the crisis was caused by a product defect, poor management decisions, or unethical behavior, owning up to mistakes can go a long way toward rebuilding trust. The public appreciates honesty and accountability, and a genuine apology can often soften the blow of a crisis.

However, taking responsibility should always be followed by action. Simply saying "we're sorry" without concrete steps to address the issue may come across as insincere. Companies must demonstrate that they are committed to making things right—whether that involves compensating affected customers, disciplining employees involved in the crisis, or implementing new policies to prevent future occurrences.

Steps to Rebuild Trust with Stakeholders

After the immediate crisis has been managed, the long-term process of rebuilding trust begins. This process is often much more challenging than damage control, as it requires companies to prove their commitment to change over an extended period.

1. Open Communication and Transparency

Transparency is key to rebuilding trust after a crisis. Stakeholders want to know what went wrong, how it happened, and what steps are being taken to prevent it from happening again. Open communication—both internally with employees and externally with customers and investors—helps demonstrate that the company is not hiding anything and is genuinely committed to addressing the root causes of the crisis.

Take the example of PureLife Pharma, a fictional pharmaceutical company that faced a major crisis when one of its top-selling drugs was found to have harmful side effects. After recalling the drug, the company held multiple public forums where senior executives answered questions directly from the public and investors. They also published a detailed investigation report outlining the steps they were taking to improve their drug testing and safety protocols. This level of transparency helped restore some of the lost trust and allowed stakeholders to feel involved in the recovery process.

2. Engage with Affected Stakeholders

If the crisis directly impacted specific groups—such as customers, employees, or investors—it is essential to engage with them personally. Offering compensation, assistance, or simply showing empathy can help mend damaged relationships. When stakeholders feel that the company genuinely cares about them, they are more likely to give the company a second chance.

For example, when a data breach exposed sensitive customer information at NeoBank, a large online banking platform, the company went above and beyond to address the concerns of affected customers. In addition to offering credit monitoring services, NeoBank's CEO personally reached out to key customers and held town hall meetings to address their concerns. This personal touch helped repair relationships and gave the company an opportunity to demonstrate its commitment to data security.

3. Implement Reforms and Demonstrate Change

Rebuilding trust requires more than just promises—it requires action. Companies must implement meaningful reforms that address the weaknesses exposed by the crisis. Whether it's updating internal policies, improving product quality, or strengthening oversight mechanisms, stakeholders need to see that the company is taking concrete steps to prevent a repeat of the crisis.

In the case of EcoGroves, a large agricultural company that faced public backlash after being accused of exploiting workers, the company took swift action by partnering with a leading labor rights organization to conduct an independent audit of its operations. They also overhauled their worker policies and committed to publishing annual reports on their labor practices. These actions showed that EcoGroves was not just paying lip service to the issue but was genuinely committed to changing its practices.

4. Invest in Reputation Repair

In the aftermath of a crisis, companies often need to invest in reputation repair. This can include rebranding efforts, launching new marketing campaigns, or supporting community initiatives to restore goodwill. However, these efforts must be authentic and aligned with the company's values—superficial gestures or "greenwashing" can backfire and worsen the damage.

For instance, when TechWave, a technology company, faced allegations of environmental harm from its manufacturing processes, it launched a comprehensive sustainability initiative. Rather than merely issuing a press release, TechWave invested in cleaner technologies, reduced its carbon footprint, and partnered with environmental NGOs to support reforestation projects. This long-term commitment to sustainability helped rebuild the company's reputation and reassured stakeholders that the company was serious about its environmental responsibilities.

Case Study: How ReBrand Apparel Recovered from a Reputational Crisis

In 2019, ReBrand Apparel, a global fashion company, was thriving in an industry known for rapid trends and intense competition. Founded by Karen Steele, a visionary entrepreneur, ReBrand had built its brand around inclusivity, sustainability, and fair labor practices. Their clothes were celebrated not just for their design but for their ethical production methods. The company prided itself on transparency, often sharing behind-the-scenes stories of the artisans who crafted their products.

However, ReBrand's reputation was severely tested when an investigative journalist published a report revealing that one of its overseas suppliers was using child labor. The news came as a shock to both the company and the public. While ReBrand was unaware of the supplier's practices, the public was quick to associate the company with unethical labor practices. Protests erupted, celebrities began boycotting the brand, and social media was flooded with negative posts condemning ReBrand.

The Crisis Unfolds

At first, ReBrand's management was slow to respond. The company issued a brief statement denying any knowledge of the child labor practices, but this only angered the public further. It seemed like ReBrand was trying to shift the blame, rather than take responsibility for its supply chain.

Recognizing the need for a more robust response, Karen Steele personally stepped in. She called an emergency meeting with her team and devised a plan to address the crisis head-on. Steele issued a public apology, taking full responsibility for the oversight and acknowledging the company's failure to monitor its suppliers closely enough. She announced that ReBrand would immediately terminate its relationship with the supplier and launch an internal investigation into its entire supply chain.

Rebuilding Trust

Steele knew that words alone wouldn't be enough to restore ReBrand's reputation. She set about implementing sweeping changes across the company. First, ReBrand hired an independent auditing firm to review its entire supply chain and publicly released the results. The company also implemented stricter monitoring and oversight mechanisms, ensuring that all suppliers complied with ReBrand's ethical labor standards.

Steele personally visited key manufacturing locations and shared updates with the public through video messages, giving stakeholders a behind-the-scenes look at the reforms being implemented. ReBrand also launched a new initiative to invest in education for children in the communities where its suppliers were based, demonstrating its long-term commitment to improving conditions in its supply chain.

The Long Road to Recovery

It took time, but slowly, ReBrand began to regain public trust. Customers appreciated the company's transparency and the steps it took to ensure the crisis wouldn't happen again. Sales eventually rebounded, and by 2021, ReBrand was once again viewed as a leader in ethical fashion. The crisis served as a turning point for the company, pushing it to live up to its brand promise more fully than ever before.

Restoring reputation after a crisis is never easy, and there are no quick fixes. However, by taking responsibility, being transparent, and implementing real change, companies can rebuild trust and emerge stronger on the other side. In the end, a company's ability to recover from a reputational crisis depends on its willingness to address the underlying issues and demonstrate to stakeholders that it is committed to doing better. ReBrand Apparel's recovery shows that, with the right approach, even the most severe reputational crises can be overcome.

Part 5:
Managing Operational Crises

Chapter 11: Navigating Operational Failures

Operational crises are an inevitable part of running a business. They can range from supply chain disruptions to product malfunctions or even workplace accidents. When these crises occur, they not only disrupt the day-to-day operations of a company but can also erode customer confidence, impact employee morale, and cause significant financial losses. While no business is immune to operational failures, how an organization navigates through such crises determines its ability to recover and thrive.

In this chapter, we will explore the causes of operational crises, their impact on business operations, and the strategies companies can use to contain and mitigate their effects. We will also present a detailed case study of a fictional manufacturing plant that successfully contained an operational disaster and emerged stronger in the aftermath.

Operational Crises: Causes and Their Business Impact

Operational crises can arise from various sources, including human error, equipment malfunctions, natural disasters, or unforeseen external factors like political instability. Regardless of their cause, these crises have the potential to bring a business to a standstill. Understanding the root causes of operational failures is essential to managing them effectively.

1. Human Error

Human error is one of the most common causes of operational crises. Mistakes made by employees—whether due to lack of training, miscommunication, or negligence—can lead to significant disruptions in operations. For example, a miscalculation in inventory management can cause stock shortages, or an oversight in quality control can result in a defective product reaching the market. While human error is often inevitable, companies can minimize its occurrence by investing in robust training programs and creating a culture of accountability.

Consider the case of Vantage Technologies, a tech firm that experienced a critical operational failure due to a data entry mistake. A simple error in inputting client information caused a massive delay in their product delivery, leading to multiple contract breaches and significant client dissatisfaction. The error was traced back to an undertrained employee who hadn't been fully versed in the company's new data management system.

2. Equipment and System Failures

Equipment breakdowns and system failures are other common causes of operational crises. In industries that rely heavily on machinery—such as manufacturing, logistics, and construction—a single machine failure can halt an entire production line. Similarly, a malfunctioning IT system can disrupt essential business processes, such as communication, order processing, and customer service. Preventive maintenance, regular system updates, and contingency planning can reduce the likelihood of such failures.

Dexla Motors, a car manufacturing company, faced a major operational crisis when a key piece of its assembly line equipment broke down unexpectedly.

The machine, which was responsible for installing crucial safety components, was offline for two weeks, leading to delays in production. Dexla Motors learned that the machine hadn't been properly maintained, and a minor mechanical issue that could have been fixed easily escalated into a major breakdown.

3. Supply Chain Disruptions

In today's interconnected global economy, many companies rely on complex supply chains that span multiple countries and regions. A disruption in one part of the supply chain—whether due to political instability, natural disasters, or logistical issues—can have a ripple effect throughout the entire organization. For example, a delay in receiving raw materials can halt production, while transportation issues can prevent finished products from reaching customers on time.

During the COVID-19 pandemic, Oceanic Fashions, a global apparel brand, experienced significant supply chain disruptions when their primary textile supplier in Southeast Asia was forced to shut down due to lockdown measures. This disruption caused production delays and missed delivery deadlines, resulting in a backlog of orders and mounting customer complaints. The company realized that its over-reliance on a single supplier made it vulnerable to external shocks and needed to diversify its supply chain network.

4. Accidents and Natural Disasters

Operational failures can also result from accidents or natural disasters that are beyond a company's control. Fires, floods, and industrial accidents can destroy physical infrastructure, harm employees, and bring operations to a halt. In such cases, companies must have contingency plans in place to protect both their people and their assets.

In 2021, BlueSky Chemicals, a chemical manufacturing company, experienced a severe operational crisis when a fire broke out in one of their production plants. The fire caused significant damage to the plant's machinery and infrastructure, halting production for several weeks. Fortunately, the company's robust emergency response plan, which included regular fire drills and evacuation protocols, ensured that all employees were safely evacuated, minimizing the potential for injury. However, the financial impact of the crisis was substantial, as the company had to invest heavily in rebuilding and restoring operations.

Crisis Management for Supply Chain Disruptions, Product Failures, and Accidents

Managing operational crises requires a swift and coordinated response. The key to successfully navigating such crises lies in preparedness, communication, and adaptability. Companies must have well-documented crisis management plans that outline the steps to be taken in the event of different types of operational failures.

1. Managing Supply Chain Disruptions

Supply chain disruptions can severely impact a company's ability to meet customer demand and maintain its market position. To mitigate the effects of supply chain failures, companies must have a robust risk management strategy in place. This includes diversifying suppliers, maintaining safety stock, and using predictive analytics to identify potential risks before they escalate.

When InnovateTech, a leading electronics manufacturer, faced a sudden disruption in its semiconductor supply chain due to geopolitical tensions, the company's risk management strategy paid off. InnovateTech had established relationships with multiple suppliers across different regions, allowing it to pivot quickly to alternative sources of raw materials. While the crisis still caused delays, the company was able to maintain production levels and meet most of its customer commitments.

2. Containing Product Failures

When a product failure occurs, the priority must be to contain the damage and protect the company's reputation. Companies should act quickly to recall defective products, offer compensation to affected customers, and communicate transparently about the issue. Internal investigations should be launched immediately to determine the root cause of the failure and implement corrective actions to prevent it from recurring.

In 2020, Sparrow Home Goods, a furniture manufacturer, experienced a crisis when one of their popular chairs was found to have a structural flaw that posed a safety risk to customers. The company acted swiftly by issuing a product recall, offering full refunds, and apologizing to customers through multiple channels, including social media and email. Sparrow Home Goods also conducted an internal investigation and introduced stricter quality control measures to ensure that future products met safety standards. While the crisis caused a temporary dip in sales, the company's proactive approach helped restore customer trust.

3. Addressing Accidents and Workplace Safety Issues

Workplace accidents can have severe consequences for both employees and the company. In the event of an accident, the safety and well-being of employees should be the top priority. Companies should have emergency response protocols in place, as well as a clear communication plan to inform employees, stakeholders, and the public about the incident.

After an explosion at Lunar Construction, a building materials company, the company's crisis management plan was immediately put into action. Emergency services were called, employees were evacuated, and the company's crisis communication team began working to keep stakeholders informed. In the aftermath of the accident, Lunar Construction provided financial assistance to injured workers and their families, while also launching a thorough investigation to identify safety gaps and implement stronger safety protocols. By demonstrating care for its employees and taking decisive action, the company was able to manage the reputational fallout from the accident.

Case Study: Containing an Operational Disaster in a Manufacturing Plant

In the summer of 2022, Atlas Manufacturing, a global leader in the production of heavy machinery, experienced one of the worst operational disasters in its 50-year history. The company's flagship plant, located in a remote industrial zone, suffered a catastrophic equipment failure that halted production for nearly a month. The incident not only impacted the company's production schedule but also threatened its long-standing reputation for reliability and quality.

The Incident

The crisis began when a critical piece of machinery on the plant's main production line malfunctioned, causing a dangerous buildup of pressure within the system. The malfunction led to a small explosion that damaged several other machines on the line and rendered the entire production floor inoperable. Fortunately, no employees were injured in the explosion, but the financial losses were immediate. The plant was responsible for producing a majority of Atlas's most popular products, and with production halted, the company faced the risk of losing key contracts with international clients.

The Response

Atlas Manufacturing's senior leadership convened an emergency crisis team within hours of the incident. The company's CEO, Frank Reynolds, led the response, ensuring that all employees were evacuated safely and medical attention was provided to those in the vicinity of the explosion. The crisis team's first task was to assess the damage and communicate with clients, employees, and other stakeholders about the situation.

Frank Reynolds understood that communication was key to preventing further reputational damage. The company issued a public statement within 24 hours of the explosion, explaining the cause of the malfunction and assuring stakeholders that a full investigation was underway. Atlas Manufacturing also provided regular updates to its clients, many of whom were worried about delayed orders.

Containment and Recovery

In the days following the incident, Atlas Manufacturing's operations team worked around the clock to repair the damaged equipment and restore production. Recognizing the urgency of the situation, the company brought in engineers from multiple global locations to expedite the repairs. Simultaneously, Atlas developed a temporary contingency plan to shift some of its production to other facilities to minimize delays.

In addition to managing the operational aspects of the crisis, Atlas Manufacturing also took steps to rebuild trust with its employees. The company provided counseling services for workers who were traumatized by the explosion and held regular town hall meetings to keep them informed about safety measures and the progress of repairs.

The company completed the necessary repairs in three weeks—one week ahead of the original timeline—and resumed full production shortly thereafter. Atlas Manufacturing's swift and transparent response earned praise from both employees and clients. While the crisis resulted in temporary production delays, the company's proactive approach to communication and recovery minimized long-term reputational damage.

Navigating operational failures requires a blend of technical expertise, clear communication, and leadership. Whether a company is dealing with supply chain disruptions, product failures, or workplace accidents, the key to crisis management is preparation and the ability to respond swiftly and effectively. As demonstrated by Atlas Manufacturing, a well-coordinated response not only mitigates the immediate impact of an operational crisis but also reinforces trust and loyalty among stakeholders. In the end, how a company manages operational failures often determines its long-term success.

Chapter 12: Crisis Planning for Operational Stability

Crisis planning is essential for any organization seeking long-term success and stability. Operational stability refers to a company's ability to maintain consistent and efficient functioning, even in the face of unexpected disruptions. Without proper planning and resilience-building, businesses can face catastrophic consequences during a crisis—be it a supply chain disruption, a product recall, or a sudden drop in demand. However, with adequate preparation, companies can mitigate damage, recover faster, and even come out stronger.

In this chapter, we will examine how businesses can create operational resilience through strategic planning and process improvement. We will also explore the tools available for managing supply chain disruptions and ensuring operational continuity. The chapter concludes with an in-depth case study of a company that successfully restructured its operations during a significant crisis, ensuring long-term stability.

Creating Operational Resilience Through Planning and Process Improvement

Operational resilience is the capacity of an organization to adapt and continue functioning during a crisis. Building such resilience requires careful planning and a commitment to continuous process improvement. The ultimate goal is to create a system that can absorb shocks, recover quickly, and maintain the ability to deliver products and services with minimal disruption.

1. Identifying Vulnerabilities

The first step in building operational resilience is identifying the vulnerabilities within your organization. This could include reliance on a single supplier, outdated technology, or inefficient processes that could be bottlenecks during a crisis. By conducting a thorough risk assessment, businesses can pinpoint where they are most vulnerable and develop targeted strategies to mitigate these risks.

For instance, Greenfield Energy, a renewable energy company, conducted a risk assessment and discovered that it was overly reliant on a single supplier for its specialized solar panels. Recognizing the risk of a supply chain breakdown, Greenfield Energy diversified its supplier base, securing agreements with additional manufacturers across multiple regions. This proactive approach allowed the company to reduce the risk of production delays and shortages, even when geopolitical tensions temporarily disrupted its primary supplier.

2. Process Standardization and Automation

Standardizing and automating processes is another critical aspect of operational resilience. When processes are standardized, businesses can ensure that tasks are completed consistently and efficiently, even during periods of crisis. Automation can help reduce human error and improve the speed and accuracy of tasks, allowing organizations to continue operating smoothly when resources are stretched.

Metro Logistics, a third-party logistics company, faced repeated operational challenges due to inconsistent processes across its multiple warehouse locations. To address this, the company implemented a standardized operations manual and invested in automation technologies, such as automated inventory management systems and robotic pickers. When a sudden surge in demand occurred during the holiday season, Metro Logistics was able to scale operations quickly without compromising on accuracy or efficiency, thanks to its streamlined processes.

3. Agile and Flexible Workforce

An agile workforce is another key component of operational resilience. Companies that cross-train employees and encourage flexibility are better equipped to handle crises. When a crisis strikes, employees may need to take on different roles, adapt to new processes, or work remotely. Businesses that invest in training and empower employees to be adaptable are more likely to maintain operational stability.

During a global pandemic, RapidMed Pharmaceuticals faced an operational crisis when a portion of its workforce fell ill, leaving critical production lines understaffed. However, because the company had invested in cross-training its employees, workers from less critical departments were able to step in and keep production running. RapidMed's commitment to workforce agility allowed it to maintain operational continuity, meet customer demand, and avoid the financial losses that would have resulted from production shutdowns.

Tools for Managing Supply Chain Disruptions and Operational Continuity

Managing supply chain disruptions is one of the biggest challenges businesses face during a crisis. With global supply chains growing increasingly complex, a breakdown at any point—whether it's a supplier shutdown, transportation delays, or raw material shortages—can have far-reaching effects on the entire operation. Companies that proactively manage their supply chains and have continuity plans in place are better positioned to withstand these disruptions.

1. Supply Chain Mapping

A critical tool for managing supply chain disruptions is supply chain mapping. This involves mapping out every step in the supply chain, from raw material suppliers to final delivery, to identify potential points of failure. By gaining visibility into the entire supply chain, businesses can detect vulnerabilities and make contingency plans to address disruptions.

ValenTech Electronics, a consumer electronics manufacturer, used supply chain mapping to identify that its lithium-ion battery supplier was located in a region prone to political instability. To mitigate the risk of supply chain disruptions, ValenTech established alternative sources for its battery supply and created an emergency stockpile. When the original supplier was forced to shut down due to civil unrest, ValenTech was able to seamlessly transition to its backup supplier, avoiding production delays.

2. Inventory Buffers and Safety Stock

Inventory buffers, also known as safety stock, are an important tool for maintaining operational continuity. By holding additional inventory of critical components or raw materials, companies can continue production even when there are temporary supply chain disruptions. However, maintaining safety stock comes with costs, so businesses need to balance the benefits of additional inventory against the financial implications.

Highline Apparel, a mid-sized clothing manufacturer, implemented a safety stock strategy for its most critical raw materials, including fabrics and zippers, after experiencing repeated supply chain disruptions during the pandemic. While maintaining extra stock increased holding costs, it also ensured that the company could continue production during supplier delays. This approach paid off when a key fabric supplier failed to deliver due to shipping issues, allowing Highline to continue producing its clothing lines without interruption.

3. Diversification of Suppliers

Diversifying suppliers is another key strategy for managing supply chain risk. Instead of relying on a single supplier for a critical component or material, businesses should establish relationships with multiple suppliers across different regions. This way, if one supplier is disrupted, the company can pivot to another supplier and continue operations without major delays.

Solarex Energy Solutions, a renewable energy company, sourced its photovoltaic cells from a single supplier in East Asia. After repeated shipping delays and disruptions caused by the pandemic, Solarex made the strategic decision to diversify its supplier base. The company now sources photovoltaic cells from multiple suppliers in Asia, Europe, and North America. This diversification not only reduced supply chain risk but also improved the company's bargaining power with its suppliers.

4. Business Continuity Planning (BCP)

A robust Business Continuity Plan (BCP) is essential for managing operational stability during a crisis. A BCP outlines how a business will continue to operate during and after a crisis, detailing steps for maintaining critical functions, safeguarding assets, and ensuring the well-being of employees. BCPs should be updated regularly and tested through crisis simulation exercises to ensure their effectiveness.

Sterling Financial Services, a financial advisory firm, had a comprehensive BCP in place when a severe hurricane struck its main office in Florida. The plan included provisions for remote working, data backups, and alternative office locations. While the physical office was heavily damaged by the storm, Sterling was able to continue its operations without interruption by shifting to remote work and relocating some critical functions to its backup office in another state. The company's proactive planning not only safeguarded its assets but also maintained its clients' trust during the crisis.

Case Study: Operational Restructuring During a Crisis

In 2019, Everline Industries, a medium-sized manufacturing company, faced one of the most challenging periods in its 80-year history. Specializing in producing industrial equipment, Everline's operations were severely impacted by a combination of supply chain disruptions, outdated processes, and an economic downturn. These factors led to major delays in product delivery, dissatisfied customers, and a steep decline in revenue. Faced with a potential collapse, Everline's leadership realized that operational restructuring was the only way to survive the crisis.

The Crisis

The root of the crisis lay in Everline's over-reliance on a single supplier for its key components, coupled with inefficient production processes that had not been updated for over a decade. When the supplier was forced to shut down due to a natural disaster, Everline's production ground to a halt. Compounding the problem, the company's manual processes were slow, and a lack of automation meant that scaling operations quickly to meet new demand was impossible.

Customer complaints started to pile up as delivery timelines were missed, and Everline's largest clients began to consider shifting their business to competitors. The company's financial losses mounted, and within months, Everline was facing bankruptcy unless drastic action was taken.

The Response

Everline's CEO, Margaret Stevens, took swift action by appointing an operational crisis team to oversee the company's restructuring. Recognizing that the company's survival hinged on more than just restoring production, Stevens and her team set out to rebuild the business from the ground up.

The first step was addressing the supply chain vulnerabilities. Everline diversified its supplier base, partnering with multiple global and local suppliers to ensure that future disruptions could be managed. This move provided the company with greater flexibility in sourcing materials and improved its bargaining power.

Next, Everline invested heavily in upgrading its production processes. The company automated several key functions, including inventory management and quality control, to reduce human error and speed up production. At the same time, Stevens restructured the workforce, cross-training employees so that they could take on multiple roles if needed. This allowed the company to remain agile and responsive to fluctuating demand.

The Recovery

The restructuring plan was not without its challenges. The initial costs of upgrading technology and implementing new processes were high, and the company had to borrow heavily to fund the changes. However, the results were quickly visible. Production times decreased by 30%, error rates dropped significantly, and customer satisfaction began to recover.

In the aftermath of the restructuring, Everline Industries not only survived the crisis but thrived. The company expanded its client base, thanks in part to its improved operational efficiency and ability to meet tighter deadlines. Everline's story is a testament to the power of proactive crisis planning and operational resilience in the face of adversity.

Crisis planning for operational stability is not a one-time effort but a continuous process that requires foresight, investment, and adaptability. As demonstrated by Everline Industries, businesses that proactively identify vulnerabilities, standardize processes, and invest in automation are better equipped to withstand crises. Additionally, managing supply chain risks through diversification and safety stock ensures continuity, even in the most challenging circumstances. In the end, the ability to recover and adapt from an operational crisis defines a company's long-term resilience and success.

Part 6:
Case Studies on Leadership During Crisis

Chapter 13:
Case Study 1- Leadership Through a Merger Crisis

Mergers and acquisitions (M&As) can be one of the most complex and anxiety-inducing events for a company. The integration of two organizations often leads to widespread uncertainty, not only for employees but also for the market and external stakeholders. Concerns over job security, organizational culture shifts, and the potential for financial instability can create a tense atmosphere that requires exceptional leadership. This case study explores how a leadership team successfully navigated the significant challenges posed by a high-profile merger, focusing on how they managed employee anxiety and market uncertainty. The lessons learned from this crisis offer valuable insights into effective leadership and communication during times of corporate upheaval.

The Situation: A Merger with High Stakes

In 2018, GlobalTech Solutions, a large multinational IT services firm, announced its intention to merge with a competitor, InfoPro Systems, in a deal worth $4.5 billion. The merger was driven by a need to consolidate resources, expand into new markets, and reduce operational redundancies in response to increasing competition in the technology sector. However, while the deal made sense from a strategic standpoint, the announcement triggered a wave of anxiety among employees and uncertainty in the market.

The news of the merger created immediate unrest within both organizations. Employees at GlobalTech feared that the integration would result in mass layoffs, particularly as there were overlapping roles and departments between the two companies. Additionally, there were concerns about how the corporate cultures of GlobalTech and InfoPro, which were markedly different, would align. InfoPro had a more laid-back, flexible approach to work, while GlobalTech was known for its structured, hierarchical environment.

The market responded nervously as well. Investors were unsure how the two companies would come together, and competitors started spreading rumors that the merger was a sign of weakness, casting doubt on the future stability of both firms. As stock prices for both companies dipped, stakeholders began questioning whether the merger was a smart move or a costly miscalculation.

Against this backdrop of uncertainty, it was clear that the leadership teams from both companies needed to act swiftly to regain control of the narrative, reassure employees, and stabilize the market perception. The situation required not only effective crisis leadership but also a transparent and well-planned communication strategy.

Leadership in Action: Managing Employee Anxiety

The leadership team, spearheaded by GlobalTech's CEO, Robert Carmichael, recognized that the first step in navigating the crisis was to address the growing anxiety among employees. If the internal culture was not stabilized, it would lead to lower morale, decreased productivity, and the potential loss of valuable talent, many of whom were already being approached by competitors looking to poach key staff during the turmoil.

1. Transparent Communication

Carmichael and his team understood that transparency was key to rebuilding trust. Within days of the merger announcement, a town hall meeting was organized where the leadership of both GlobalTech and InfoPro addressed employees directly. The town hall was broadcast to offices worldwide, ensuring that every employee, from senior managers to junior staff, had access to the same information.

During the meeting, Carmichael was candid about the challenges ahead but emphasized the long-term benefits of the merger. He assured employees that job redundancies would be kept to a minimum and that those affected would receive ample support in transitioning to new roles, either within the merged company or elsewhere. He also announced the creation of a task force dedicated to employee welfare during the merger, which included representatives from both companies to address concerns and ensure that employee voices were heard.

This open communication approach was a stark contrast to the norm in many mergers, where employees are often left in the dark until decisions are made. By being transparent about the uncertainties while also outlining the steps being taken to mitigate negative impacts, Carmichael was able to reduce panic and prevent a mass exodus of talent.

2. Empowering Middle Management

Carmichael knew that leadership could not resolve every issue from the top down. Therefore, the next crucial step was to empower middle managers—the ones who had the most direct contact with employees and were best positioned to manage day-to-day concerns.

A leadership summit was held where all department heads and middle managers from both GlobalTech and InfoPro were brought together to align on the company's new vision. At this summit, middle managers were given training on change management, particularly in how to handle difficult conversations about potential layoffs, role changes, and shifts in organizational culture. They were also tasked with regularly holding smaller, department-specific meetings to maintain an open line of communication with their teams.

3. Supporting Employee Well-Being

As part of its employee-centric approach, GlobalTech introduced several initiatives aimed at reducing stress and supporting employee well-being. A 24/7 counseling hotline was established, where employees could confidentially discuss their concerns with professional counselors. Additionally, leadership promoted a "flexibility guarantee," allowing employees to adjust their work hours or work remotely as they adapted to the changes brought on by the merger. By acknowledging the emotional impact of the merger, GlobalTech's leadership fostered a sense of empathy that helped employees feel more secure in an otherwise uncertain environment.

Stabilizing the Market: Managing Public Perception

While addressing internal concerns was vital, the leadership team also had to manage the external narrative. Stock prices for both companies had dropped, and market analysts were raising questions about the feasibility of the merger.

1. Controlling the Media Narrative

To regain control of the public narrative, Carmichael and InfoPro's CEO, Angela Carter, took a proactive approach to media relations. Rather than wait for speculation to spiral out of control, they organized a joint press conference to present a unified front and share the rationale behind the merger. They clearly outlined how the combined company would be better positioned to serve clients, enter new markets, and leverage complementary strengths in technology innovation and customer service.

In addition to the press conference, a media campaign was launched that included interviews with key leadership figures and articles in respected business publications, emphasizing the long-term vision and growth prospects of the merger. By addressing concerns directly and painting a clear picture of the benefits, the leadership team was able to shift the market narrative from one of fear to one of opportunity.

2. Engaging Investors and Stakeholders

Carmichael and Carter also prioritized communication with major investors and other external stakeholders. They held several private meetings with institutional investors and key clients to address their concerns directly, providing them with detailed integration plans and reassuring them that their investments were safe. This helped to quell some of the panic in the market and prevented further drops in stock prices.

Additionally, the leadership team worked with industry analysts to present detailed financial models showing the anticipated cost savings and growth opportunities that would arise from the merger. These proactive steps helped restore confidence in both companies and demonstrated that leadership had a clear plan for making the merger a success.

Outcome: Lessons Learned from Effective Crisis Leadership

The merger between GlobalTech Solutions and InfoPro Systems was not without its challenges, but the leadership team's approach ultimately proved effective. Within a year of the merger, the combined company had stabilized its workforce, regained investor confidence, and successfully integrated its operations. Stock prices recovered, and the company emerged as a stronger competitor in the IT services market.

Several key lessons can be drawn from this case study:

1. Transparency Is Key

One of the most significant factors in the leadership team's success was their commitment to transparency. By openly acknowledging the uncertainties and challenges of the merger, they were able to build trust with employees and external stakeholders alike. This open communication strategy prevented the situation from spiraling into panic and allowed the leadership team to maintain control of the narrative.

2. Empowerment at All Levels

The leadership team's decision to empower middle managers to take an active role in communicating with employees was another critical success factor.

These managers were better positioned to understand and address the concerns of their teams, allowing for more effective crisis management on the ground. Empowering leaders at all levels of the organization is essential for navigating large-scale changes.

3. Emotional Intelligence Matters

Finally, the leadership team's focus on employee well-being showed a high degree of emotional intelligence. By offering counseling services and flexible work arrangements, they acknowledged the human side of the crisis and demonstrated that they valued their employees not just as workers, but as individuals. This approach not only helped retain talent but also contributed to a more positive work environment during the transition.

Leadership through a merger crisis requires a combination of transparency, empathy, and proactive communication. The case of GlobalTech Solutions and InfoPro Systems illustrates how addressing both internal and external concerns with a clear, strategic approach can lead to a successful outcome, even in the face of significant uncertainty. Through effective crisis leadership, organizations can emerge from such disruptions stronger, more resilient, and better positioned for future growth.

Chapter 14: Case Study 2- Crisis in the Digital Age: Cybersecurity Breach

The digital age has transformed the way businesses operate, but it has also made them more vulnerable to cybersecurity threats. A cyber breach can have devastating consequences, not only in terms of data loss but also in the erosion of trust from customers, stakeholders, and employees. This case study explores how a major financial services company, NeXtrel Capital, faced a significant cybersecurity breach that compromised sensitive data. The story of how the leadership team responded to the breach, contained the damage, restored trust, and ultimately strengthened the company's cybersecurity systems offers a detailed look at crisis management in the digital age.

The Situation: A Major Cybersecurity Breach

In the fall of 2020, NeXtrel Capital, a prominent global financial services firm, faced a cybersecurity nightmare. The company, which managed millions of individual and corporate accounts, discovered that its internal network had been infiltrated by a sophisticated hacking group. Over a period of several weeks, the hackers had accessed sensitive information, including personal details, financial data, and even confidential communications with high-profile clients. The breach was not only an internal disaster but also a legal and public relations crisis waiting to unfold.

The attack was detected when an internal security audit flagged unusual activity in NeXtrel's client databases. Upon further investigation, the cybersecurity team realized that the hackers had already exfiltrated large amounts of data, including account numbers, Social Security information, and sensitive investment profiles. The situation was dire: if the data leak became public, it could destroy the company's reputation, cause severe financial loss, and result in legal action from clients.

Despite their immediate efforts to isolate the compromised systems, the breach had already caused significant damage. NeXtrel's leadership team, led by CEO Jonathan McAllister and CTO Emily Lin, had to act swiftly to contain the crisis and mitigate the fallout. The company had a strong digital security framework in place, but this breach demonstrated the vulnerability even the most prepared companies can face. The stakes were enormous. Trust was the backbone of NeXtrel's business model, and if clients lost faith in the company's ability to protect their data, the consequences would be catastrophic.

Leadership in Action: Containing the Breach and Communicating Transparently

The first step for NeXtrel's leadership team was containment. Emily Lin, as CTO, spearheaded the technical response. She immediately convened the company's cybersecurity incident response team and brought in outside cybersecurity experts to assist with the investigation and remediation.

1. Containment of the Breach

One of the initial steps taken by Lin and her team was to isolate all compromised systems. This included shutting down affected servers, blocking unauthorized access points, and fortifying any vulnerabilities identified in the network. While the internal cybersecurity team worked on closing the gaps, the external consultants provided an unbiased analysis of the situation. They identified that the breach was initiated through a phishing attack targeting a mid-level employee, followed by an escalation of privileges that gave the hackers administrative access to the network.

While the technical team worked to contain the breach, CEO Jonathan McAllister focused on communication. He knew that the longer NeXtrel remained silent, the worse the fallout would be. Rather than waiting for rumors to spread or for the breach to be exposed by the media, McAllister made a bold decision: to go public with the breach within 48 hours of its discovery.

2. Transparent Communication with Clients and the Public

In a carefully crafted public statement, McAllister informed the company's clients and stakeholders about the breach, its potential impact, and the steps the company was taking to address the situation. His message was clear: while NeXtrel's systems had been compromised, the company was doing everything in its power to contain the damage and ensure that clients' funds and personal information would be protected. He offered full transparency, stating that while the investigation was ongoing, clients would be kept updated regularly.

The leadership's decision to communicate quickly and honestly set NeXtrel apart from other companies that had faced similar breaches. While some companies might have tried to hide the breach for as long as possible, NeXtrel's transparency earned them immediate goodwill, even in the face of such a negative event. Although clients were understandably concerned, McAllister's openness about the breach reassured many that the company was handling the situation responsibly.

NeXtrel also set up a dedicated hotline and online portal for affected clients, giving them direct access to customer service representatives who could answer questions about the breach and provide guidance on how to protect their accounts.

Rebuilding Trust: Engaging Clients and Strengthening Security

In the days following the breach, NeXtrel's leadership team recognized that the real challenge lay ahead. Containing the breach was only the first step; rebuilding trust with clients and stakeholders required a multi-faceted strategy.

1. Offering Compensation and Support

To show their commitment to their clients, NeXtrel offered immediate compensation to those affected by the breach. The company offered free credit monitoring and identity theft protection services to all clients, regardless of whether their data had been compromised. For high-net-worth individuals and corporate clients, NeXtrel went even further by offering financial reimbursement for any direct losses resulting from the breach, up to a certain amount.

In addition, McAllister personally reached out to NeXtrel's largest clients, holding one-on-one meetings to reassure them that the company was taking every possible step to secure their data and prevent future breaches. This direct engagement with top clients was a critical move, as these clients represented a significant portion of NeXtrel's assets under management. By taking a personal approach to communication, McAllister helped rebuild trust and prevent clients from jumping ship to competitors.

2. Strengthening Cybersecurity Measures

At the same time, CTO Emily Lin and her team launched an aggressive campaign to strengthen NeXtrel's cybersecurity infrastructure. Working alongside the external cybersecurity experts, they conducted a comprehensive audit of the company's systems, identifying any remaining vulnerabilities and implementing new protocols to prevent future attacks.

Among the measures introduced were multi-factor authentication (MFA) across all employee accounts, enhanced encryption for client data, and more rigorous internal training on phishing and other common cyberattack vectors. Additionally, Lin implemented a real-time monitoring system that would alert the cybersecurity team to any suspicious activity, allowing for faster detection and response in the event of another breach.

NeXtrel also made the decision to hire a Chief Information Security Officer (CISO), a newly created role, to oversee the company's cybersecurity strategy going forward. The CISO reported directly to the CEO, signaling to clients and stakeholders that cybersecurity was now a top priority at the highest levels of leadership.

Outcome: Emerging Stronger from the Crisis

Over the course of several months, NeXtrel Capital worked diligently to rebuild its reputation and reinforce its cybersecurity posture. Though the initial fallout from the breach was significant, with a temporary drop in stock prices and a handful of clients choosing to leave the firm, the majority of NeXtrel's clients remained loyal, thanks in large part to the company's transparent communication and swift action.

In fact, by the end of the fiscal year, NeXtrel had not only recovered but had also experienced growth in client acquisition. The company's proactive approach to cybersecurity and the visible steps it took to protect its clients earned it praise in the industry. Several industry analysts cited NeXtrel as a model of how to handle a cybersecurity crisis, and the company was even able to leverage its experience to improve its marketing narrative, positioning itself as a leader in cybersecurity and data protection.

Key Lessons Learned:

1. Transparency is Essential

NeXtrel's decision to go public with the breach early on was a crucial factor in minimizing the damage to its reputation. By being upfront about the issue and keeping clients informed throughout the process, the company was able to maintain a level of trust that would have been impossible had they waited or tried to conceal the breach.

2. Swift and Decisive Action

The leadership team's swift response to the breach—both in terms of containment and communication—was instrumental in preventing the situation from spiraling out of control. Their quick action not only mitigated the damage but also reassured clients that the company was capable of handling such crises effectively.

3. Building Stronger Systems Post-Crisis

Finally, NeXtrel's commitment to strengthening its cybersecurity infrastructure after the breach helped ensure that the company emerged stronger from the crisis. Rather than simply addressing the immediate problem, the leadership team took the opportunity to overhaul their security systems and protocols, which ultimately led to greater long-term resilience.

The NeXtrel Capital cybersecurity breach is a powerful example of how a major digital crisis can be managed effectively through transparent communication, quick action, and a commitment to long-term improvements. The company's leadership demonstrated that even in the face of a potentially devastating cyberattack, it is possible to not only contain the damage but also rebuild trust and emerge stronger than before. In the digital age, where cybersecurity threats are a constant risk, the ability to manage such crises with competence and integrity is more important than ever.

Chapter 15: Case Study 3- Ethical Crisis: Navigating Corporate Scandals

In today's business environment, corporate scandals can erupt at any moment, causing immense damage to a company's reputation, profitability, and employee morale. These ethical crises often catch organizations off-guard, placing leadership under intense scrutiny from both internal and external stakeholders. The way leadership handles such scandals not only defines the company's future but also sends a strong message about its commitment to ethical behavior and transparency.

This chapter examines the ethical crisis faced by Solarya Global, a multinational energy corporation, when it was discovered that senior executives had been involved in a major corruption scandal. The case illustrates how leadership, led by CEO Martha Torres, navigated the crisis and restored public trust through decisive action, transparency, and a renewed focus on corporate ethics.

The Situation: A Corruption Scandal Unfolds

Solarya Global was a global leader in renewable energy, highly respected for its commitment to environmental sustainability and innovation. Its market reputation was stellar, and its commitment to clean energy made it a favorite of socially responsible investors. However, in 2022, a scandal broke that threatened to shatter the company's reputation.

An anonymous whistleblower within the company leaked documents to a major investigative news outlet, alleging that several top executives in Solarya's Latin American division had been involved in bribery and illegal kickbacks to secure lucrative government contracts. The documents included evidence of secret payments made to officials in multiple countries over several years, violating international anti-corruption laws, including the U.S. Foreign Corrupt Practices Act (FCPA).

The news sent shockwaves through the energy industry. Solarya Global, a company known for its ethical business practices, was now accused of engaging in serious corruption. The company's stock price plummeted, investors panicked, and media outlets around the world questioned how such a scandal could have occurred within a firm that had always portrayed itself as a beacon of corporate responsibility.

CEO Martha Torres, who had taken the helm only a year earlier, found herself facing the biggest crisis of her career. The public and investors demanded answers, employees were demoralized, and the company faced potential legal repercussions that could cripple its operations. Torres had to act quickly and decisively to prevent Solarya from losing the trust of its stakeholders entirely.

Leadership's Response: Addressing the Crisis Head-On

Martha Torres understood that in ethical crises, the biggest mistake a company can make is attempting to downplay or cover up the situation. Instead, she opted for a strategy of complete transparency and a zero-tolerance policy on corruption, no matter how high the scandal reached within the organization.

1. A Swift and Transparent Internal Investigation

Torres' first move was to commission an independent, third-party investigation into the allegations. She hired an external law firm with no previous ties to the company to ensure impartiality. This investigation was tasked with uncovering the full extent of the wrongdoing, identifying all individuals involved, and providing recommendations on how to prevent such incidents in the future. By bringing in external auditors, Torres sent a clear message that she was committed to rooting out corruption, regardless of how damaging the findings might be.

The results of the investigation were worse than initially thought. It was revealed that not only had senior executives in the Latin American division engaged in illegal practices, but certain middle managers across different regions had also been implicated in the scheme. The investigation also revealed gaps in Solarya's internal controls and compliance procedures that had allowed these unethical practices to go unchecked for years.

Despite the damning results, Torres chose not to hide the findings. Instead, in a public statement, she revealed the full scope of the investigation, shared the company's failings, and laid out a comprehensive plan to address the issues.

2. Publicly Addressing the Crisis

Within days of the investigation's conclusion, Torres held a press conference, flanked by the company's legal team and newly appointed Chief Ethics Officer, Jeremy Carver. She openly acknowledged the company's ethical failures and took full responsibility as CEO, even though the corruption had occurred before her tenure began. She emphasized that Solarya Global was committed to fixing the problems and restoring trust. Her speech was heartfelt and direct:

"We have failed in our duty to uphold the highest ethical standards that we, as a company, have always stood for. This is not who we are or who we aspire to be. We are taking immediate action to correct these wrongs and rebuild the trust we have lost. To those who have been affected by this, I offer my deepest apologies."

Torres's transparency in admitting the company's wrongdoing was a risky move, but it was one rooted in her understanding that the public values accountability. She refused to shift blame or make excuses, which set her apart from leaders who, in similar crises, often tried to deflect responsibility.

Restoring Ethics and Rebuilding Trust: Comprehensive Reforms

After the initial shock of the scandal and the public apology, Torres and her leadership team turned their attention to fixing the deeper issues that had allowed the corruption to take place. They implemented several key measures aimed at restoring ethics within the company and rebuilding the trust of both employees and external stakeholders.

1. Firing and Restructuring

The most immediate action was the termination of all individuals involved in the scandal, regardless of their rank or contributions to the company. This included several high-profile executives in Solarya's Latin American division who had been with the company for decades. Although this was a difficult decision—especially given some of these individuals' roles in growing the business—Torres was adamant that Solarya could not tolerate corruption at any level.

In addition to firing those directly involved in the scandal, Torres ordered a complete restructuring of the company's compliance department. Jeremy Carver, the newly appointed Chief Ethics Officer, was given full authority to overhaul Solarya's internal controls and compliance mechanisms. Carver immediately began to strengthen the company's anti-corruption training programs, mandating that all employees, regardless of rank, undergo intensive training on ethical decision-making, corporate governance, and legal compliance.

2. Implementing New Governance and Compliance Systems

Under Carver's leadership, Solarya implemented a comprehensive governance overhaul. This included:

- ✓ **A whistleblower protection program**: One of the most significant changes was the creation of an internal whistleblower program, which allowed employees to report unethical practices anonymously. The company also established an independent ethics committee that reported directly to the board of directors, ensuring that whistleblower reports would be taken seriously and acted upon without fear of retaliation.
- ✓ **Stricter compliance audits**: Solarya began conducting regular, unannounced compliance audits across all of its divisions. These audits were designed to identify potential ethical risks before they became full-blown scandals. The audits were overseen by an external firm to maintain objectivity.

- ✓ **Enhanced transparency in financial reporting**: Solarya took steps to improve transparency in its financial reporting processes. This included more detailed disclosures in its public filings, particularly in areas related to government contracts and payments made to third-party contractors. The company also began publishing an annual ethics and compliance report, detailing its efforts to prevent corruption and other unethical behaviors.

3. Engaging Employees and Clients in the Reform Process

Restoring trust internally was just as important as regaining public confidence. Torres and her leadership team knew that many employees were demoralized by the scandal, so they took an active approach to engaging staff in the reform process. This included town hall meetings where employees could voice their concerns and ask questions directly to the leadership team.

In addition, the company rolled out a series of interactive workshops that allowed employees to discuss real-world ethical dilemmas and how they would respond to them in their roles. This hands-on approach helped reinforce the importance of ethics in everyday decision-making.

Externally, Torres met with key clients and investors to personally reassure them of the company's commitment to transparency and ethical practices. She outlined the steps the company was taking to prevent future scandals and emphasized the importance of ethics to the long-term health of the business.

Outcome: Restoring Trust and Emerging Stronger

Over the next two years, Solarya Global managed to restore its reputation, thanks in large part to the decisive actions taken by Torres and her leadership team. The company regained the trust of its stakeholders through transparency, accountability, and a renewed commitment to ethical business practices.

Key Outcomes:

- ✓ **Rebuilt Client and Investor Confidence**
  Despite an initial dip in stock prices, Solarya's public commitment to ethics and transparency won back the trust of major clients and investors. Several socially responsible investment firms that had considered divesting after the scandal instead reaffirmed their commitment to Solarya, citing the company's genuine efforts to reform.
- ✓ **Stronger Internal Culture**
  Internally, employee engagement surveys conducted after the scandal showed that Solarya's workforce had regained confidence in the company's leadership. Employees reported a stronger sense of pride in working for a company that took its ethical responsibilities seriously. The new whistleblower protections also encouraged a culture of openness, where employees felt more comfortable reporting unethical behavior without fear of retribution.
- ✓ **Recognition as an Industry Leader in Ethics**
  Two years after the crisis, Solarya was recognized by several industry watchdogs and

governance organizations for its efforts to improve corporate governance and ethical practices. The company's annual ethics and compliance report became a benchmark for other firms in the energy sector, and Solarya's experience was frequently cited as a case study on how to manage corporate scandals effectively.

Key Leadership Lessons:

1. Transparency and Accountability are Non-Negotiable

Martha Torres's decision to publicly acknowledge the company's ethical failings was the turning point in this crisis. Her refusal to downplay the scandal or shift blame allowed Solarya to begin rebuilding trust immediately.

2. Ethics Must Be Embedded in Every Layer of the Organization

The reforms implemented after the scandal showed that ethics cannot simply be a top-down mandate; they must be embedded in the company culture, from senior executives to entry-level employees. Solarya's new training programs, governance structures, and whistleblower protections ensured that ethics were a part of everyday decision-making.

3. Crises Can Be Opportunities for Growth

While the scandal initially seemed catastrophic, Solarya emerged from the crisis stronger than ever. By addressing its ethical weaknesses head-on, the company not only regained public trust but also built a stronger internal culture that was more resilient to future challenges.

Through this case study, we learn that leadership during an ethical crisis requires courage, transparency, and a long-term vision for ethical growth. Martha Torres's leadership at Solarya Global provides a blueprint for how to manage corporate scandals without losing public trust—and, ultimately, how to emerge stronger from them.

Chapter 16:
Case Study 4- Supply Chain Disruptions

In the modern globalized economy, businesses are increasingly dependent on complex supply chains that span multiple countries and continents. A disruption in any part of the supply chain can send shockwaves through the entire organization, leading to significant operational and financial losses. TransVelo Logistics, a leading manufacturer of electric bicycles, faced such a crisis in 2020 when a sudden disruption in its supply chain threatened to halt its production and jeopardize its relationships with major retailers.

The Situation: A Sudden Disruption

TransVelo Logistics had a well-established supply chain, sourcing components from several suppliers across Asia. The company was experiencing rapid growth, with increasing demand for electric bicycles from eco-conscious consumers in Europe and North America. However, in early 2020, a key supplier in Vietnam suddenly ceased operations due to political unrest in the region. This supplier was responsible for manufacturing critical battery components, and without them, TransVelo could not meet its production targets.

The timing of the disruption could not have been worse. TransVelo was in the midst of negotiations with several major retailers for a new line of electric bicycles set to be launched in the upcoming holiday season. If the company failed to deliver the products on time, it risked losing the contracts, damaging its reputation, and potentially facing financial ruin.

Leadership's Response: Building Resilience

CEO Daniel Mayer understood the gravity of the situation. Rather than panic or shift blame to external forces, he took immediate action to mitigate the crisis. Mayer and his leadership team initiated a three-pronged approach to resolve the supply chain disruption and prevent future issues.

1. Identifying Alternative Suppliers

Mayer immediately tasked the company's procurement team with finding alternative suppliers for the battery components. Within two weeks, they had identified a reliable supplier in South Korea. Although this supplier's components were slightly more expensive, Mayer made the decision to prioritize speed and quality over cost. By negotiating an expedited production schedule, TransVelo was able to minimize delays.

2. Strengthening Supplier Relationships

Mayer recognized that the company's over-reliance on a single supplier had been a significant vulnerability. To address this, he initiated a diversification strategy, building stronger relationships with multiple suppliers across different regions. He personally met with potential suppliers to discuss long-term partnerships that would ensure stable production, even in the face of geopolitical disruptions.

3. Implementing a Digital Supply Chain Platform

In parallel, the company invested in a digital supply chain management platform that provided real-time visibility into every aspect of the supply chain. This system allowed TransVelo to monitor potential risks in advance, such as supplier delays, shipping issues, and geopolitical instability. The platform also allowed for better communication with suppliers, ensuring that issues could be addressed before they escalated into crises.

Outcome: Preventing Future Disruptions

While the initial disruption delayed production by three weeks, Mayer's swift actions ensured that TransVelo met its commitments to major retailers. The company successfully launched its new product line during the holiday season, and thanks to its enhanced supply chain resilience, it continued to grow rapidly in the years that followed. By diversifying its supply base and investing in digital tools, TransVelo became a model of supply chain resilience in the electric vehicle industry.

Chapter 17:
Case Study 5- Global Pandemic Crisis

When the COVID-19 pandemic erupted in early 2020, businesses around the world faced unprecedented challenges. For WellCare Pharma, a mid-sized pharmaceutical company specializing in non-critical medications, the pandemic represented both a logistical nightmare and an opportunity to redefine its business model. The company's supply chains were disrupted, production plants were closed, and employee safety became a paramount concern.

The Situation: A Pandemic-Induced Crisis

WellCare Pharma was highly dependent on imports of raw materials from China and India, both of which were among the countries hardest hit by the pandemic in its early stages. Lockdowns and restrictions led to severe delays in shipments of key ingredients, halting production at WellCare's factories in the U.S. and Europe.

Simultaneously, the pandemic had heightened demand for certain medications, while reducing the need for others. WellCare's primary product line—a range of anti-allergy and digestive medications—was not in high demand compared to essential medicines like ventilators or anti-viral drugs. The company was at risk of losing significant market share to competitors who were better positioned to respond to the pandemic.

Leadership's Response: Pivoting and Prioritizing Employee Safety

Under the leadership of CEO Rashid Jaffer, WellCare Pharma adopted a flexible and adaptive approach to the pandemic. Rather than waiting for the crisis to pass, Jaffer's leadership team made bold decisions that helped the company weather the storm.

1. Pivoting to Critical Products

One of the first steps Jaffer took was to pivot the company's manufacturing capabilities toward producing essential medical supplies that were in high demand during the pandemic. WellCare began producing personal protective equipment (PPE), including face masks and hand sanitizers, leveraging its existing production lines to shift toward critical products. This allowed the company to remain operational and serve public health needs.

2. Protecting Employees and Ensuring Operational Continuity

Employee safety became a top priority for Jaffer, especially as several workers at the company's manufacturing plants tested positive for COVID-19. Jaffer implemented stringent safety protocols, including socially distanced workstations, regular testing, and providing PPE for all employees. He also initiated flexible work arrangements, allowing non-essential employees to work from home while providing additional hazard pay for workers who continued to report to the factories.

3. Building a Pandemic-Resilient Supply Chain

To address the disruption in raw material supply, Jaffer led efforts to diversify WellCare's supply chain. By sourcing ingredients from multiple countries and building relationships with local suppliers, the company ensured that it would not face similar delays in the future. WellCare also developed stockpiles of critical materials to prepare for future disruptions.

Outcome: Emerging Stronger

While WellCare Pharma, like many companies, faced significant challenges during the pandemic, its quick pivot to essential products and its focus on employee safety allowed it to weather the crisis. In fact, by the end of 2021, the company had not only recovered its market position but also expanded into new product lines, including protective equipment and disinfectants. The pandemic became a catalyst for long-term growth and innovation at WellCare Pharma.

Chapter 18:
Case Study 6- Workplace Safety and Compliance Issues

In industries where physical labor is required, workplace safety is paramount. IronBridge Construction, a construction firm specializing in large infrastructure projects, faced a major crisis in 2018 when a serious workplace accident occurred on one of its sites, resulting in the injury of several workers. The accident led to intense scrutiny from regulators and the media, and IronBridge's leadership had to act swiftly to prevent long-term damage to its reputation and operations.

The Situation: A Workplace Accident

IronBridge Construction had earned a reputation as one of the safest companies in the construction industry, with stringent safety protocols in place. However, during the construction of a major bridge in the city of Havenbrook, a scaffolding collapse resulted in the injury of five workers, two of whom were critically injured.

The accident immediately drew the attention of the media, government regulators, and labor unions. There were questions about whether IronBridge had failed to follow safety protocols, and several employees at the site accused the company of cutting corners to meet tight deadlines. IronBridge faced potential legal penalties, as well as a significant blow to its reputation.

Leadership's Response: Prioritizing Transparency and Safety

CEO Nathan Whitlock took full responsibility for the crisis and immediately prioritized the safety of all employees. Whitlock recognized that the company's response to the accident would determine whether it could retain the trust of its workers and clients.

1. Immediate Investigation and Safety Overhaul

Whitlock ordered a full, independent investigation into the cause of the scaffolding collapse. This investigation was conducted by a third-party engineering firm, and the findings were made public in order to maintain transparency. The investigation revealed that while the company's safety protocols had been followed in most areas, a lapse in supervision on the day of the accident contributed to the incident.

In response, Whitlock ordered a company-wide safety overhaul. He introduced stricter safety training programs for all employees, including mandatory refresher courses for supervisors and site managers. Additionally, he increased the number of safety inspectors on all construction sites to ensure compliance with protocols at all times.

2. Open Communication with Stakeholders

Whitlock understood that transparency was critical to maintaining trust. He held regular meetings with employees, unions, and regulators, updating them on the progress of the investigation and the steps IronBridge was taking to improve safety. By keeping an open line of communication, Whitlock ensured that all stakeholders felt informed and reassured.

3. Supporting Injured Workers and Families

Whitlock also made it a priority to support the workers who had been injured in the accident. He personally visited them in the hospital and offered financial assistance to cover their medical bills. The company also provided counseling services to the families of the injured workers and offered long-term rehabilitation support for those who needed it.

Outcome: A Culture of Safety

The scaffolding accident could have been a major blow to IronBridge's reputation, but Whitlock's transparent and compassionate response helped the company recover. By prioritizing safety and investing in new training programs, IronBridge became a leader in workplace safety in the construction industry. The company's accident rate fell by 40% in the following two years, and its commitment to safety was recognized by several industry bodies.

Chapter 19: Case Study 7- Market and Economic Volatility

In 2019, Bevera Foods, a mid-sized beverage company, found itself in a precarious situation as market volatility and rising raw material costs threatened its profitability. The company, known for its line of organic fruit juices, relied heavily on imports of exotic fruits from South America. However, due to a combination of adverse weather conditions, trade disputes, and economic downturns, the cost of these imports skyrocketed, putting immense pressure on Bevera's bottom line.

The Situation: Economic Turbulence

Bevera Foods had built its brand around offering premium, organic fruit juices that were both healthy and ethically sourced. However, as the cost of imported fruits rose sharply, the company was forced to consider raising prices or finding alternative suppliers. Neither option was ideal. Increasing prices risked alienating the company's loyal customer base, while switching to lower-quality ingredients would undermine its brand image.

To make matters worse, economic uncertainty in key markets, including Europe and North America, further exacerbated the situation. Consumers were cutting back on discretionary spending, and Bevera's sales began to decline.

Leadership's Response: Adaptation and Innovation

CEO Michelle Albright realized that Bevera could not afford to wait out the economic turbulence. Instead, the company needed to adapt and find innovative solutions to preserve its market position and profitability.

1. Diversifying the Product Line

Albright spearheaded a strategic initiative to diversify Bevera's product line. The company introduced a new range of more affordable, locally sourced juices that appealed to cost-conscious consumers. These products used fruits grown domestically, reducing Bevera's reliance on expensive imports. At the same time, the company maintained its premium organic line, ensuring that it could cater to both budget-conscious and high-end consumers.

2. Operational Efficiency and Cost Reduction

Albright also led efforts to improve operational efficiency across the company. Bevera streamlined its supply chain, reducing waste and cutting transportation costs. Additionally, the company invested in more sustainable packaging, which not only reduced costs but also resonated with eco-conscious consumers. These efforts helped to offset the rising costs of raw materials and improve profitability.

3. Strengthening the Brand's Ethical Appeal

Recognizing that consumers were becoming more value-conscious during the economic downturn, Bevera doubled down on its commitment to ethical sourcing and sustainability. Albright launched a marketing campaign that highlighted the company's partnerships with fair-trade farmers and its use of eco-friendly packaging. This helped to differentiate Bevera from competitors and retain its loyal customer base, even as economic conditions worsened.

Outcome: Navigating Volatility Successfully

Despite the challenges posed by market volatility, Bevera Foods emerged from the crisis stronger and more resilient. The company's diversified product line allowed it to appeal to a wider range of consumers, while its commitment to ethical sourcing and sustainability helped to solidify its brand identity. Bevera's ability to adapt quickly to changing market conditions allowed it to weather the economic storm and position itself for long-term growth.

Chapter 20: Case Study 8- Environmental Disasters

In 2017, TerraGreen Energy, a renewable energy company, faced an environmental crisis when one of its wind farms was struck by a major natural disaster—a Category 5 hurricane that devastated the southern coast of the United States. The hurricane caused widespread damage to TerraGreen's wind turbines, resulting in millions of dollars in losses and raising questions about the company's preparedness for extreme weather events.

The Situation: A Natural Disaster Strikes

TerraGreen Energy had built a reputation as a pioneer in the renewable energy sector, with wind farms located in several regions known for their abundant wind resources. The company's largest wind farm, located near the coastal town of Bayshore, was a critical part of its energy production capacity.

When Hurricane Isaac struck the region, it caused unprecedented damage to the wind farm. Several turbines were destroyed, and the farm was forced to shut down for repairs. The disaster led to significant financial losses for TerraGreen and raised concerns about the vulnerability of renewable energy infrastructure to extreme weather events.

Leadership's Response: Rebuilding and Future-Proofing

CEO Emma Collins was faced with the dual challenge of repairing the damage caused by the hurricane while also ensuring that TerraGreen's operations could withstand future environmental disasters. Collins and her leadership team developed a comprehensive response plan that focused on rebuilding the wind farm and enhancing the company's resilience to extreme weather.

1. Rapid Response and Community Engagement

Collins understood that TerraGreen's response to the disaster would be closely scrutinized by both the public and investors. She quickly mobilized resources to begin repairs on the damaged wind farm, working closely with local authorities and emergency response teams. Collins also ensured that TerraGreen provided financial assistance to the residents of Bayshore, many of whom had been affected by the hurricane. By engaging with the community and offering support, TerraGreen strengthened its relationship with the local population.

2. Investing in Climate-Resilient Infrastructure

In the aftermath of the hurricane, Collins led an initiative to invest in more climate-resilient infrastructure. TerraGreen worked with engineers to redesign its wind turbines, making them more resistant to high winds and extreme weather conditions. The company also developed new protocols for shutting down turbines in advance of major storms, minimizing damage during future disasters.

3. Collaborating with the Renewable Energy Industry

Recognizing that extreme weather events posed a growing threat to the entire renewable energy sector, Collins took a leadership role in advocating for industry-wide solutions. TerraGreen collaborated with other renewable energy companies, government agencies, and environmental organizations to develop best practices for protecting renewable energy infrastructure from environmental disasters.

Outcome: Leading the Industry in Climate Resilience

TerraGreen Energy's response to Hurricane Isaac positioned the company as a leader in climate resilience within the renewable energy sector. By investing in more resilient infrastructure and advocating for industry-wide solutions, TerraGreen not only rebuilt its wind farm but also set a new standard for how renewable energy companies can prepare for the increasing frequency of extreme weather events. The company's proactive approach allowed it to recover from the disaster and emerge as a stronger, more resilient organization.

Chapter 21: Case Study 9- Legal and Regulatory Crises

In 2016, MedicaLife, a healthcare technology company that specialized in developing software for hospitals and clinics, found itself embroiled in a legal and regulatory crisis when one of its products was accused of violating patient privacy laws. The software, which was designed to help healthcare providers store and manage patient records, had inadvertently exposed sensitive patient data, leading to multiple lawsuits and regulatory investigations.

The Situation: A Data Breach and Regulatory Scrutiny

MedicaLife's flagship product, HealthSecure, had been widely adopted by hospitals and clinics across the country. However, a flaw in the software's encryption system led to the accidental exposure of thousands of patient records, including personal health information. The breach was discovered by a third-party security firm, which reported it to the authorities.

The data breach sparked outrage among patients, healthcare providers, and regulators. MedicaLife was hit with multiple lawsuits from affected patients, and the company faced a major investigation by the Health and Data Protection Authority (HDPA), which had the power to impose significant fines for violations of privacy laws.

Leadership's Response: Restoring Trust and Compliance

CEO Jonathan Quinn recognized that the data breach represented an existential threat to MedicaLife. If the company failed to address the issue quickly and transparently, it risked losing the trust of its customers and facing crippling legal penalties.

1. Immediate Transparency and Apology

Quinn took swift action by publicly acknowledging the data breach and issuing an apology to the affected patients and healthcare providers. He emphasized that MedicaLife took full responsibility for the incident and was committed to addressing the underlying issues. Quinn's decision to be transparent from the outset helped to mitigate some of the backlash from the media and customers.

2. Strengthening Data Security

MedicaLife immediately partnered with leading cybersecurity experts to overhaul its data security protocols. Quinn personally oversaw the development of a new encryption system that provided enhanced protection for patient records. The company also implemented regular security audits to ensure that its software met the highest standards for data protection.

3. Cooperation with Regulators

Rather than adopting an adversarial stance toward regulators, Quinn made it a priority to cooperate fully with the HDPA investigation. MedicaLife worked closely with regulators to demonstrate that the company was taking meaningful steps to improve its data security and prevent future breaches. This cooperative approach helped to reduce the severity of the penalties imposed by the HDPA.

Outcome: A Stronger Commitment to Privacy

While the data breach was a significant setback for MedicaLife, the company's proactive response allowed it to restore trust with its customers and regulators. By investing in stronger data security measures and demonstrating a commitment to transparency, MedicaLife was able to emerge from the crisis with its reputation intact. The company's experience also served as a wake-up call for the entire healthcare technology industry, highlighting the importance of robust data protection in an increasingly digital world.

Chapter 22:
Case Study 10- Technological Crises – AI Mismanagement

As artificial intelligence (AI) becomes an integral part of many industries, the potential for technological crises has grown. In 2021, InnoData, a data analytics firm, experienced a major crisis when an AI algorithm it had developed for a financial services client produced biased and inaccurate results, leading to significant financial losses for the client and a reputational crisis for InnoData.

The Situation: AI Gone Wrong

InnoData had been hired by a major investment firm, ClearStone Capital, to develop an AI-driven tool that could analyze market trends and make investment recommendations. However, shortly after the tool was deployed, ClearStone Capital began to experience significant financial losses. An internal investigation revealed that the AI algorithm had been trained on biased data, leading it to make faulty investment recommendations that disproportionately favored certain industries over others.

The crisis not only led to a loss of millions of dollars for ClearStone Capital but also raised serious questions about the ethical and technical oversight of InnoData's AI development process. The company faced legal threats from its client and a wave of negative publicity.

Leadership's Response: Ethical AI and Accountability

CEO Daniel Redding understood that the crisis had exposed deep flaws in InnoData's approach to AI development. To recover from the crisis, Redding and his leadership team had to address both the technical and ethical issues at the heart of the problem.

1. Conducting an Ethical Review of AI Practices

Redding immediately commissioned an independent review of InnoData's AI development practices. The review, conducted by a team of external experts, identified several areas where the company's processes had failed, including insufficient oversight of training data and a lack of attention to potential biases. Redding made the results of the review public, signaling the company's commitment to transparency and accountability.

2. Retraining the AI Model

InnoData worked with ClearStone Capital to retrain the AI model using a more diverse and representative dataset. The company also implemented new guidelines for data collection and algorithm development to ensure that future AI tools would be free from bias and meet the highest ethical standards.

3. Establishing an AI Ethics Board

To prevent similar issues in the future, Redding established an internal AI ethics board responsible for reviewing all AI projects and ensuring that they met the company's ethical and technical standards. The board included experts in AI, data ethics, and compliance, and it was tasked with providing ongoing oversight of InnoData's AI initiatives.

Outcome: Leading in AI Ethics

While the AI mismanagement crisis was a major setback for InnoData, the company's response positioned it as a leader in the emerging field of ethical AI development. By taking responsibility for the crisis and implementing meaningful reforms, InnoData was able to rebuild its reputation and restore trust with its clients. The company's experience also served as a reminder to the tech industry of the importance of ethical oversight in AI development, particularly as AI plays an increasingly central role in business decision-making.

Each of these case studies underscores the importance of effective leadership, transparency, and innovation in crisis management. From supply chain disruptions and legal crises to environmental disasters and AI mismanagement, these examples illustrate the complex challenges that organizations face in today's rapidly changing world. Leaders who are proactive, adaptable, and committed to ethical practices are best positioned to navigate these crises and emerge stronger on the other side.

Part 7:
Building a Resilient Organization Post-Crisis

Chapter 23: Post-Crisis Evaluation and Learning

Crises can be defining moments for organizations, often revealing weaknesses in their operations, leadership, and planning. However, these moments also present invaluable opportunities to learn, improve, and fortify the organization against future disruptions. For a business to emerge stronger from a crisis, it must undergo a structured evaluation of what transpired, identify both successes and failures, and translate those insights into long-term strategies. This chapter explores how companies can effectively conduct post-crisis evaluations and how such learning can be embedded into the organization's culture for future resilience.

Conducting Post-Crisis Reviews: What Went Right and Wrong

One of the most critical steps after managing a crisis is conducting a thorough post-crisis review. This reflective process allows the company to analyze its response, assess its effectiveness, and develop insights to better prepare for future challenges. Without this step, an organization risks repeating the same mistakes, while also missing the opportunity to capitalize on what was done correctly.

A well-executed post-crisis review involves examining three key areas:

1. Crisis Preparedness:

How well was the organization prepared for the crisis? This involves looking at whether there were pre-existing contingency plans, whether those plans were adequate for the situation, and how quickly they were activated. Many companies are caught off guard because their plans either do not exist or are outdated, leaving them scrambling to react.

2. Crisis Response:

The crisis response should be reviewed from multiple angles. How quickly did the leadership team act? Were employees well-informed and involved in the process? Did communication channels function effectively both internally and externally? Successful companies respond to crises with coordination, but weaknesses often surface in real-time, exposing communication breakdowns, delays in decision-making, or confusion in the chain of command.

3. Post-Crisis Adaptation:

The organization must also examine how well it adapted after the immediate crisis subsided. Were recovery plans initiated quickly and effectively? Did the company engage in rebuilding or strengthening relationships with stakeholders? Was there clear accountability for the actions taken during the crisis?

For instance, consider HarperTech, a mid-sized software development firm that faced a major cybersecurity attack that compromised their clients' data. While HarperTech had a cybersecurity response plan in place, the company failed to adapt quickly to the scope of the breach. Their technical teams were overwhelmed, communication between departments was weak, and external communication with clients was delayed and incomplete, leading to loss of trust and several clients pulling their business. A post-crisis review revealed that the organization's response plan was outdated, and many employees were unclear about their roles in the crisis, highlighting a need for a more robust crisis preparedness plan and more thorough employee training.

Learning From Failures and Successes:

HarperTech's post-crisis evaluation underscored both failures and successes. While their IT response team eventually managed to stop the breach, the success was overshadowed by communication failures that damaged their relationships with clients. Through the post-crisis review, HarperTech implemented a cross-functional crisis management team, mandated crisis communication drills, and updated its cybersecurity protocols. Learning from both what went right and what went wrong can lead to comprehensive organizational improvement.

Embedding Crisis Management into the Company's Culture

To create a resilient organization, crisis management must become an integral part of the company's DNA rather than an isolated function activated only during emergencies. A company that embeds crisis management into its culture operates proactively, always anticipating potential risks and being prepared to act when necessary. This kind of preparedness and adaptability must be instilled across every level of the organization, from leadership to frontline workers.

Building a Culture of Resilience:

Crisis management should not merely be a top-down initiative, where only the C-suite is involved in crisis planning. It needs to be a company-wide commitment, with every employee understanding their role in preventing, responding to, and recovering from crises. Continuous training and simulations can play a crucial role in embedding this into the company's daily operations.

Take the example of Stratford Logistics, a global shipping and logistics company that was impacted by severe disruptions during a global pandemic. Stratford had some crisis management protocols in place, but the sheer scale of the pandemic caught the company off-guard. After struggling to maintain its operations for the first few months, the company realized that crisis management needed to be a core competency embedded in every department and at every level.

Long-Term Embedding of Crisis Management:

Stratford's leadership launched a company-wide resilience initiative. This included:

- ✓ **Crisis Response Training for All Employees:** Every employee, from warehouse workers to executives, was trained on crisis management principles specific to their roles. These trainings were regularly refreshed and included simulated exercises that tested response times and decision-making under pressure.
- ✓ **Cross-Department Collaboration:** Stratford established dedicated crisis management teams composed of representatives from different departments, ensuring that there was expertise and leadership distributed throughout the organization. In the event of another crisis, each department was empowered to respond swiftly and autonomously rather than waiting for centralized instructions.
- ✓ **Scenario Planning and Simulations:** One key learning from Stratford's experience was

the importance of scenario planning. The company worked with risk management experts to identify potential future crises—ranging from natural disasters to political instability in key shipping regions—and conducted regular simulations to ensure preparedness.

By making crisis management a permanent part of its culture, Stratford was able to create a more adaptable organization that could respond quickly to future disruptions. As a result, during a later regional port strike, Stratford was able to reroute shipping operations smoothly, avoiding major losses.

Real-Life Example: Post-Crisis Transformation at Vendale Global

The story of Vendale Global, a fictitious international consumer goods company, illustrates how an organization can undergo a complete transformation following a crisis, emerging stronger than before.

The Crisis:

In 2020, Vendale Global faced a significant reputational crisis when reports surfaced that several of their factories in Southeast Asia were involved in unethical labor practices, including poor working conditions and underpayment of workers. News of the scandal spread rapidly, and the company found itself under intense media scrutiny and public backlash. Customers began boycotting Vendale's products, and several key retail partners severed ties with the company. The scandal also triggered regulatory investigations, threatening heavy fines and legal repercussions.

Vendale's initial response was slow and defensive, further aggravating public outrage. The company's leadership team was unprepared for the scope of the crisis and struggled to manage the flow of negative information. Sales plummeted, and internal morale reached an all-time low. The company was at a tipping point, with many questioning whether it could recover.

The Post-Crisis Review and Transformation:

Realizing the gravity of the situation, Vendale's newly appointed CEO, Oliver Grant, initiated a full-scale post-crisis review, inviting external consultants and engaging with internal stakeholders at all levels of the organization. The review was brutally honest, identifying major gaps in corporate governance, supply chain oversight, and crisis communication. The company also recognized the need to rebuild its brand from the ground up, starting with a commitment to ethical practices.

Instead of viewing the crisis as an isolated incident, Grant saw it as a turning point for the company. Vendale embarked on a transformative journey with three core pillars:

- ✓ **Supply Chain Transparency:** Vendale introduced a radical level of transparency in its supply chain, allowing consumers to track where each product was sourced and how it was made. The company worked closely with non-profit organizations and local governments to ensure that all factories adhered to ethical labor standards. This not only restored consumer trust but also set a new benchmark in the industry for corporate responsibility.
- ✓ **Crisis Communication and Leadership:** The crisis had revealed that Vendale's leadership team was unprepared to handle public

relations disasters. To address this, Grant implemented leadership development programs focused on crisis communication, decision-making under pressure, and stakeholder engagement. The company also created a crisis communication task force to ensure that future issues would be addressed swiftly and transparently.

- ✓ **Embedding Ethical Practices into the Culture:** Recognizing that the crisis had deeper cultural roots, Grant worked to shift Vendale's corporate culture from a profit-first mentality to a people-first approach. Employee training programs were redesigned to include ethical decision-making, and performance metrics were adjusted to reflect not only financial success but also social and environmental impact. Vendale also established a new governance structure that included an independent ethics board responsible for ensuring that the company adhered to its stated values.

Outcome:

Within two years, Vendale Global had regained much of its lost market share, and its reputation had been rebuilt around a new ethical and transparent business model. The company's stock price, which had plummeted during the crisis, steadily climbed as investors regained confidence in Vendale's leadership and future prospects. By turning the crisis into an opportunity for growth and learning, Vendale had transformed itself into a more resilient, responsible, and sustainable organization.

Conclusion: The Path to Long-Term Resilience

The most successful organizations are those that not only manage crises effectively but also learn from them and embed that learning into their culture. Post-crisis reviews are essential in identifying both strengths and weaknesses in an organization's response, while embedding crisis management into the company's DNA ensures long-term resilience.

Whether through continuous employee training, proactive scenario planning, or a deep commitment to transparency and ethics, companies that build a culture of crisis management are better equipped to handle the next inevitable disruption. By evaluating their actions, learning from their experiences, and making crisis management part of everyday business practice, they ensure that they will not only survive but thrive in the face of future challenges.

Chapter 24:
Templates and Tools for Crisis Management

In today's unpredictable business environment, effective crisis management can make or break an organization. Having the right templates and tools at hand allows leaders to respond swiftly and confidently during times of crisis. These resources provide a structured approach to managing unexpected disruptions, ensuring that decision-making is informed, communication is clear, and recovery is planned with precision.

This chapter offers a detailed exploration of four essential tools for crisis management: a crisis communication template for immediate response, decision-making frameworks for crisis scenarios, a scenario planning toolkit, and templates for post-crisis evaluation and recovery planning. Each tool is illustrated with detailed case studies to demonstrate how they can be effectively used in real-world situations.

Crisis Communication Template for Immediate Response

Effective communication is critical in the first moments of a crisis. Missteps, delays, or unclear messaging can exacerbate an already difficult situation, leading to confusion and loss of trust. A crisis communication template helps ensure that the organization's response is timely, consistent, and transparent. The template provides a structured guide for what to say, to whom, and when, ensuring that messaging aligns with the company's values and objectives.

Case Study: Cynerix Health Solutions

Situation:

Cynerix Health Solutions, a healthcare technology company, faced a crisis when one of their medical devices was reported to have a malfunction, leading to a patient's death in a hospital. As news spread rapidly, the company was bombarded with questions from media outlets, hospitals, and healthcare providers using their devices.

Initial Misstep:

The company's first instinct was to delay any public statements until they had more information. However, this created a vacuum, allowing rumors and misinformation to spread. By the time Cynerix issued an official statement, their reputation had already been damaged, and trust was eroded.

Using the Crisis Communication Template:

After realizing their mistake, Cynerix's leadership team turned to a pre-prepared crisis communication template. They immediately issued a clear and concise statement, acknowledging the issue, expressing empathy for the affected family, and outlining the steps they were taking to investigate the malfunction. The statement was distributed through multiple channels, including press releases, social media, and direct communication with hospitals and regulators.

Key Components of the Template:

- ✓ **Acknowledgment of the Crisis:** Cynerix acknowledged the situation within the first few sentences to show transparency and urgency.
- ✓ **Empathy and Concern:** They expressed sympathy for the family affected, ensuring

their response was humane and compassionate.

- ✓ **Actions Being Taken:** The company quickly listed the immediate steps being taken, including the recall of the device, an internal investigation, and cooperation with regulatory bodies.
- ✓ **Clear Communication Channels:** Cynerix provided contact information for customers and media to ask questions or seek updates, ensuring they controlled the narrative.

The quick implementation of this template helped stabilize the situation. While the initial misstep hurt the company's image, their subsequent transparency and swift actions reassured stakeholders that the issue was being handled responsibly.

Decision-Making Frameworks for Crisis Scenarios

In a crisis, decision-making can feel overwhelming, especially when emotions run high, and there's pressure to act swiftly. A structured decision-making framework provides clarity in chaos, guiding leaders through the process of assessing information, weighing options, and making informed choices.

Case Study: Astral Manufacturing

Situation:

Astral Manufacturing, a large industrial producer, faced a sudden labor strike after several workplace safety concerns were raised. Employees halted production, demanding immediate improvements, while customers began voicing concerns about delayed deliveries. Leadership was under pressure to address the strike quickly to resume operations, but rushing to make a decision without careful consideration could further alienate employees or customers.

The Framework in Action:

Astral's leadership team used the **DECIDE Framework**, a crisis decision-making tool designed to help evaluate options under pressure.

- ✓ **Define the Crisis:** The strike was rooted in legitimate workplace safety concerns. Leadership acknowledged that ignoring these concerns could harm employee trust and morale in the long term.
- ✓ **Evaluate Options:** The team identified several options, including continuing production with temporary workers, quickly addressing minor safety concerns to placate employees, or pausing operations to fully resolve safety issues.
- ✓ **Consider the Consequences:** They evaluated the long-term implications of each option. Temporarily using replacement workers could lead to further unrest, while addressing safety concerns comprehensively would delay production but ensure long-term stability.
- ✓ **Identify Best Solutions:** The leadership chose to prioritize employee safety and long-term trust, deciding to halt production and address all safety issues. They communicated openly with customers about the delay, ensuring transparency.
- ✓ **Develop Action Plans:** A clear timeline for implementing the safety improvements was established, and employees were informed of the specific changes being made.

- ✓ **Evaluate Results:** Over time, this decision helped restore employee morale, and customers appreciated the company's integrity, strengthening relationships.
- ✓ By following the DECIDE framework, Astral was able to navigate the crisis with clear reasoning, ensuring that short-term pain did not lead to long-term damage.

Scenario Planning Toolkit

A scenario planning toolkit allows organizations to anticipate various crises before they occur. By envisioning multiple future scenarios, leaders can prepare response strategies for each possibility, reducing the likelihood of being caught off guard. This approach is particularly valuable in industries where external factors, such as market volatility, technological disruptions, or natural disasters, can have a significant impact.

Case Study: Horizon Foods

Situation:

Horizon Foods, an international food distribution company, relies heavily on a global supply chain. With rising geopolitical tensions in several key regions, Horizon's leadership team recognized the potential for supply chain disruptions that could severely impact their ability to deliver products to customers.

Using the Scenario Planning Toolkit:

The team developed multiple scenarios, each representing different levels of disruption:

- ✓ **Mild Disruption:** Political tensions lead to slight delays in shipping from one key region.

- ✓ **Moderate Disruption:** Labor strikes in multiple countries cause significant delays in production and shipping.
- ✓ **Severe Disruption:** An international trade embargo halts all shipping from key regions, requiring the company to source ingredients from entirely new locations.

For each scenario, Horizon developed a detailed response plan, including identifying alternative suppliers, adjusting shipping schedules, and preparing communication strategies for customers.

When moderate disruptions began in one of their key regions, Horizon was able to implement their pre-planned response quickly, avoiding major impacts on their delivery schedules and maintaining customer trust. By anticipating the possibility of multiple disruptions, Horizon Foods maintained operational flexibility and resilience.

Templates for Post-Crisis Evaluation and Recovery Planning

After a crisis, it's essential for organizations to conduct thorough evaluations and develop recovery plans that not only address the immediate aftermath but also lay the foundation for long-term resilience. A structured evaluation helps identify what worked, what didn't, and how future responses can be improved. A recovery plan, meanwhile, focuses on restoring operations, rebuilding trust, and ensuring that the organization is better prepared for future disruptions.

Case Study: Luminex Enterprises

Situation:

Luminex Enterprises, a technology company specializing in renewable energy solutions, experienced a major crisis when a key supplier went bankrupt, halting the production of their flagship product. The crisis disrupted their entire supply chain, leading to missed deadlines and frustrated customers.

Using the Post-Crisis Evaluation Template:

Once the crisis was under control, Luminex conducted a detailed post-crisis evaluation to assess its response. The evaluation focused on the following areas:

- ✓ **Initial Response Effectiveness:** The review revealed that Luminex's initial reaction was delayed because of overreliance on a single supplier. The company had underestimated the importance of maintaining backup suppliers.
- ✓ **Communication Strategy:** Luminex had communicated effectively with some stakeholders, but the evaluation showed that their communication with international customers was slower than necessary, causing some damage to their relationships.
- ✓ **Supply Chain Vulnerabilities:** The evaluation identified weaknesses in their supply chain and concluded that diversification of suppliers should be a priority going forward.
- ✓ **Recovery Planning:** With these lessons in mind, Luminex developed a comprehensive recovery plan that focused on the following areas:
- ✓ **Supplier Diversification:** Luminex established partnerships with multiple suppliers to avoid dependency on any single provider.

- ✓ **Customer Communication:** The company implemented a more robust customer communication strategy to ensure faster and more transparent updates in future crises.
- ✓ **Operational Resilience:** Luminex invested in building stronger relationships with key stakeholders across their supply chain and conducted regular assessments of supplier stability.

Over the next two years, Luminex strengthened its operations and saw renewed growth. Their commitment to learning from the crisis ensured they were far better prepared for future disruptions.

Building Resilience Through Structured Crisis Management

Having the right tools and templates for crisis management allows organizations to respond swiftly, make informed decisions, and recover from disruption more effectively. Whether it's communicating transparently with stakeholders, using decision-making frameworks to evaluate options, or developing scenario plans to anticipate potential crises, these tools form the backbone of a resilient organization.

By embedding these processes into the company culture, organizations ensure that they are not just reacting to crises but proactively preparing for them. These tools, when used effectively, turn crises into opportunities for growth and improvement, making the organization stronger in the long run.

Chapter 25: Conclusion

Crisis management is more than just responding to emergencies as they arise. It is about building a resilient organizational culture that can adapt, survive, and even thrive in the face of adversity. Throughout this book, we have examined numerous real-life scenarios where companies faced significant challenges, and we've broken down how effective leadership, clear communication, and strategic decision-making made the difference between failure and recovery. In this final chapter, we will recap the key lessons learned, outline the essential steps to becoming a crisis-ready leader, and discuss how to embed resilience into an organization's DNA to ensure it can withstand future crises.

Key Takeaways: Recap of Lessons Learned from the Case Studies

The case studies presented throughout this book provide powerful insights into how different types of crises unfold and how they can be managed effectively. By examining various scenarios such as supply chain disruptions, technological failures, legal challenges, and environmental disasters, we have identified several key themes that repeatedly surface when navigating through crises.

1. The Importance of Early Preparedness

In nearly every case study, preparedness was the linchpin of a successful response. Companies that anticipated potential threats—whether through scenario planning or by developing contingency plans—were able to respond swiftly and effectively when disaster struck. For example, Horizon Foods demonstrated the value of scenario planning in Chapter 24. By preparing for multiple supply chain disruptions in advance, they were able to mitigate the impact of a labor strike that could have otherwise crippled their operations. This foresight allowed them to maintain customer trust and operational continuity.

2. Communication is Crucial

One of the most consistent findings from the case studies was the critical role of communication. Organizations that communicated transparently and proactively with stakeholders—be it employees, customers, or investors—were more likely to preserve trust and loyalty. In contrast, delays or inconsistencies in messaging often worsened the crisis. For instance, Cynerix Health Solutions in Chapter 24 learned this lesson the hard way when their initial silence allowed rumors to spread, damaging their reputation. Their eventual recovery was built on a structured, empathetic communication strategy that acknowledged the problem, outlined their response, and kept stakeholders informed throughout the resolution process.

3. Strong Leadership Makes the Difference

Leadership plays a vital role in steering an organization through crisis. The decisions made by leaders—often under immense pressure—can have long-lasting consequences. In several of the case studies, including Astral Manufacturing's response to the labor strike, we saw how thoughtful leadership, grounded in ethics and transparency, fostered trust and commitment among employees. Leaders who prioritize both the well-being of their people and the long-term viability of the company are far more successful in navigating crises than those who focus only on short-term gains.

4. Flexibility and Adaptability are Key

Rigid plans can quickly become irrelevant in a rapidly changing crisis situation. Leaders who remain adaptable, reassess conditions as they evolve, and are willing to pivot strategies were often more successful. The case of Luminex Enterprises in Chapter 24 demonstrated this well. When their key supplier went bankrupt, they initially struggled, but by conducting a thorough post-crisis evaluation and adjusting their supply chain model, they were able to recover and become more resilient in the long term.

Steps to Becoming a Crisis-Ready Leader

A crisis-ready leader is someone who not only possesses the technical skills to manage a crisis but also has the emotional intelligence to lead people through uncertainty. This type of leader combines foresight, calm under pressure, and the ability to communicate effectively with a clear focus on long-term goals. Based on the examples and lessons from this book, here are the key steps to becoming a crisis-ready leader:

1. Develop a Crisis Mindset

Crisis-ready leaders must cultivate a mindset that anticipates and prepares for potential challenges. This involves thinking through worst-case scenarios, developing response plans, and rehearsing them. Leaders should regularly assess vulnerabilities within their organization and industry, and constantly question how the organization would respond in a crisis.

2. Prioritize Transparent Communication

Being able to communicate clearly and effectively during a crisis is one of the most important leadership skills. Crisis-ready leaders are transparent with both internal and external stakeholders. They don't hide problems; instead, they address them head-on, explain the steps being taken to resolve the issue, and provide regular updates. Practicing open, empathetic communication during normal operations builds the trust that will be needed in times of crisis.

3. Lead with Empathy and Ethics

During a crisis, employees and customers will look to leaders for reassurance. Crisis-ready leaders show empathy, addressing concerns while maintaining an ethical foundation in all decisions. This ensures that both short-term decisions and long-term strategies consider the human element and build credibility and loyalty. Leaders like those at Astral Manufacturing, who focused on the well-being of employees while resolving a labor strike, show the lasting value of ethical leadership.

4. Build a Diverse and Capable Team

A strong leader understands the value of a diverse, capable team that can handle different aspects of a crisis. Crisis-ready leaders surround themselves with individuals who bring unique perspectives and skills to the table, ensuring that no potential solution or idea is overlooked. Diversity in thought leads to more innovative and effective solutions during crises.

5. Remain Calm Under Pressure

Crises often involve high-stakes decisions made under significant pressure. Leaders must maintain composure and think clearly, even in the face of uncertainty. Calm, decisive leadership provides reassurance to others and allows for more effective decision-making.

How to Build Organizational Resilience for Future Crises

Building a resilient organization requires more than just implementing crisis plans. It's about embedding crisis management into the company's culture so that every employee understands their role in a crisis and feels empowered to act. Here are some steps organizations can take to foster resilience:

1. Integrate Crisis Planning into Everyday Operations

Organizations should treat crisis preparedness as an ongoing process rather than a one-time activity. Crisis plans must be regularly reviewed, updated, and tested through simulations and drills. This ensures that the organization is always ready to respond effectively.

2. Foster a Culture of Transparency and Trust

An organization's culture plays a huge role in how it responds to crises. Companies that encourage open communication, transparency, and trust are better equipped to handle challenges. Employees should feel comfortable reporting potential issues before they escalate into full-blown crises.

3. Encourage Flexibility and Innovation

Resilient organizations are those that remain flexible and adaptable in the face of change. Encouraging innovation and creativity in problem-solving during normal operations fosters the same behavior in crisis situations. Employees should feel empowered to think outside the box and propose solutions that may not follow the usual playbook.

4. Invest in Training and Development

Continuous training ensures that employees at all levels are prepared to respond to crises. From leadership development programs to emergency response drills, organizations must invest in developing the skills and capabilities needed to handle disruptions. This not only includes technical training but also soft skills like emotional intelligence, communication, and decision-making under pressure.

5. Learn from Every Crisis

After every crisis, organizations must conduct a thorough evaluation to identify what worked and what didn't. This process, as we saw in the Luminex Enterprises case, is crucial for building resilience. By taking the time to analyze their response and make adjustments, organizations can prevent the same mistakes from being repeated in the future and become more prepared for whatever comes next.

Conclusion: Creating a Crisis-Resilient Future

As we conclude, the overarching message is clear: crises are inevitable, but failure is not. By adopting a proactive mindset, developing clear communication strategies, and learning from each crisis, organizations and leaders can emerge stronger. Building resilience is not an overnight task, but a continuous process of evaluation, adaptation, and preparation.

Leadership during a crisis is not about eliminating risk altogether, but about minimizing its impact and guiding the organization toward recovery. By following the lessons outlined in this book, any leader can develop the skills and strategies necessary to weather even the most unexpected storms, ensuring that their organization not only survives but thrives in the future.

Exercises for Readers

Different Examples of Case Studies for Different Crisis that CEO's are likely to face

These case studies present complex crises that CEOs are likely to face, requiring thoughtful and strategic responses. By discussing these scenarios, participants can engage in meaningful group discussions to analyze the situations, develop comprehensive crisis management plans, and propose viable solutions that consider long-term organizational resilience.

Case Study 1: Cybersecurity Breach

Scenario: You are the CEO of a mid-sized retail company, BlueHorizon Ltd., with both a physical and online presence. Recently, your IT team detected a major cybersecurity breach, where hackers gained unauthorized access to sensitive customer information, including credit card details. Customers are beginning to report fraudulent transactions, and the breach has already attracted media attention. The company's stock price is beginning to dip, and there are fears that this breach may lead to significant legal repercussions. You are facing growing pressure from the board of directors to handle the situation swiftly.

Guiding Questions:

- ✓ *How would you address customer concerns and restore their trust?*
- ✓ *What immediate steps would you take to mitigate the damage?*

- ✓ *How would you communicate with your internal team, shareholders, and the public?*
- ✓ *What long-term measures would you implement to prevent future breaches?*

Case Study 2: Public Relations Crisis

Scenario: As the CEO of GreenTerra Farms, a large agribusiness specializing in organic products, you face a serious issue when a popular environmental blog accuses your company of using harmful pesticides on its crops. Despite your company's commitment to sustainability, a whistleblower within the organization has provided evidence to the contrary. The story has gone viral on social media, sparking outrage among customers, environmental groups, and even some of your key retail partners.

Guiding Questions:

- ✓ *What immediate steps would you take to address the negative publicity?*
- ✓ *How would you investigate the allegations internally?*
- ✓ *What approach would you take to communicate with your stakeholders and restore your brand's credibility?*
- ✓ *What long-term changes might be necessary to repair trust with your customer base?*

Case Study 3: Leadership Scandal

Scenario: As the CEO of TechWorks Inc., you find yourself in the midst of a leadership scandal. One of your senior executives, known for their instrumental role in company growth, has been accused of unethical behavior involving insider trading. Although the allegations have not yet been proven, the executive's reputation is tarnished, and the company's integrity is being questioned. Employees are demoralized, and several investors are considering withdrawing their support.

Guiding Questions:

- ✓ *How would you manage the internal response, particularly among employees and shareholders?*
- ✓ *What steps would you take to investigate the situation and maintain transparency without jumping to conclusions?*
- ✓ *What would your communication strategy be if the executive is found guilty or innocent?*
- ✓ *How can you prevent such scandals from occurring again in the future?*

Case Study 4: Supply Chain Disruption

Scenario: You are the CEO of Apex Appliances, a global manufacturing company. Due to unforeseen geopolitical tensions between two countries critical to your supply chain, your company is facing a severe disruption in acquiring key components for its products. Production has already been delayed for two weeks, causing a backlog in orders, and you are receiving mounting complaints from customers. Your major retail partners are also threatening to drop your products unless you can guarantee consistent delivery times.

Guiding Questions:

- ✓ *What steps would you take to stabilize the supply chain in the short term?*
- ✓ *How would you manage communication with your retail partners, customers, and employees?*

- ✓ *What alternative strategies would you consider to ensure long-term supply chain resilience?*
- ✓ *How might this disruption affect the company's profitability and market reputation?*

Case Study 5: Product Recall

Scenario: As the CEO of StellarTech, a consumer electronics company, you are informed that your latest smartphone model has a critical defect in its battery, causing it to overheat and, in some cases, catch fire. Several customers have reported injuries, and there is potential for lawsuits. The news has just hit mainstream media, and your team is in panic mode. Retailers are pulling your products off the shelves, and regulatory bodies are investigating the safety of your devices. You must decide how to handle the recall and manage the fallout.

Guiding Questions:

- ✓ *What are your immediate priorities in addressing the product defect?*
- ✓ *How would you handle the recall, both logistically and in terms of public relations?*
- ✓ *How would you reassure customers and protect the company's reputation moving forward?*
- ✓ *What processes could you implement to avoid such product failures in the future?*

Case Study 6: Employee Strike

Scenario: You are the CEO of Harmony Healthcare, a large healthcare provider. Recently, your nurses and support staff have announced a strike, citing unsafe working conditions, low pay, and lack of support during high-stress periods like the pandemic.

The strike is set to begin in three days, and it threatens to disrupt critical medical services to patients. The media is already covering the story, and patient advocacy groups are beginning to take sides. Your board is concerned about the financial impact, while your HR department is urging you to find a resolution quickly.

Guiding Questions:

- ✓ *How would you balance the needs of your staff and the operational demands of your organization?*
- ✓ *What immediate steps would you take to prevent or mitigate the impact of the strike?*
- ✓ *How would you communicate with staff and the public, considering both sides of the argument?*
- ✓ *What long-term changes might be necessary to prevent such actions from occurring in the future?*

Case Study 7: Financial Crisis

Scenario: As the CEO of BrightStar Media, an entertainment company that produces popular television shows and films, you are facing a severe financial crisis. Due to a combination of poor investments, declining viewership, and a failed acquisition of a competitor, your company is on the brink of bankruptcy. You need to decide how to manage the financial situation, protect jobs, and salvage the business while dealing with anxious stakeholders and mounting debts. The board is divided on whether to declare bankruptcy or seek alternative funding.

Guiding Questions:

- ✓ *What would be your approach to stabilizing the financial situation in the short term?*
- ✓ *How would you manage internal communication to keep morale up during this difficult time?*
- ✓ *What potential rescue strategies (e.g., mergers, layoffs, seeking investors) would you consider, and how would you prioritize them?*
- ✓ *What would be your long-term strategy to restore the company's financial health?*

Case Study 8: Natural Disaster

Scenario: You are the CEO of GlobalShip, an international shipping company with operations in multiple coastal regions. Recently, a massive hurricane has struck one of your main shipping hubs, destroying warehouses and halting all operations in the region. The disaster has caused significant damage to your inventory, disrupted supply lines, and stranded several of your employees. Emergency services are stretched thin, and it could take weeks before normal operations can resume. Meanwhile, clients are demanding answers about delayed shipments and lost goods.

Guiding Questions:

- ✓ *How would you prioritize your response in the immediate aftermath of the disaster?*
- ✓ *What steps would you take to ensure the safety of your employees and secure remaining assets?*
- ✓ *How would you handle client concerns and manage expectations during this period of uncertainty?*
- ✓ *What measures would you implement to improve disaster preparedness in the future?*

Case Study 9: Executive Resignation Amid Crisis

Scenario: As the CEO of NeoVista Pharmaceuticals, you find yourself in a leadership vacuum after your Chief Operating Officer (COO) suddenly resigns amid an ongoing drug trial crisis. The drug trial, which was expected to be a game-changer for the company, has hit a roadblock as regulators are questioning the data integrity of the results. The COO, who was heavily involved in the trial, has stepped down citing "personal reasons," leading to speculation of potential wrongdoing. Investors are panicking, and the stock price is plummeting.

Guiding Questions:

- ✓ *How would you manage the leadership gap during this crisis?*
- ✓ *What steps would you take to ensure transparency and address investor concerns?*
- ✓ *How would you handle the ongoing regulatory investigation?*
- ✓ *What strategies could you implement to stabilize the company and restore confidence in leadership?*

Case Study 10: Legal and Compliance Crisis

Scenario: You are the CEO of NovaEnergy, a renewable energy company that has gained attention for its innovative wind and solar projects. However, a recent investigation has uncovered compliance violations regarding the environmental impact of one of your major projects. Regulators have issued a cease-and-desist order, and the project is now facing legal challenges from environmental groups. Your company's reputation for sustainability is at stake, and the halt in the project is costing millions in lost revenue.

Guiding Questions:

- ✓ *How would you address the legal and regulatory challenges posed by this situation?*
- ✓ *What steps would you take to manage the project's environmental impact and regain compliance?*
- ✓ *How would you communicate with stakeholders, especially investors and environmental groups, to rebuild trust?*
- ✓ *What measures could you introduce to prevent similar compliance issues in the future?*

Appendices

The following appendices provide essential tools and resources for leaders and organizations seeking to strengthen their crisis management strategies. Each template is designed to offer a practical guide for different stages of crisis response, from initial communication to post-crisis evaluation, with clear examples and detailed steps that can be tailored to various organizational needs.

Appendix 1:
Crisis Communication Plan Template

A well-structured communication plan is crucial for ensuring that stakeholders are kept informed and reassured during a crisis. This template provides a framework for organizing communication efforts in a structured, clear, and timely manner. The goal of this plan is to minimize confusion, control the narrative, and maintain trust with internal and external stakeholders.

1. Situation Overview

The communication plan starts with a brief description of the crisis situation. This section outlines what has happened, how it occurred, and what the initial response is.

Example: On January 5th, 2023, Metroline Logistics suffered a cyberattack that compromised its customer data. Hackers gained access to personal and financial information of over 200,000 customers. Immediate actions were taken to contain the breach and notify affected customers.

2. Objectives

The objectives section should clearly define what the organization hopes to achieve with its crisis communication efforts.

Example:

Ensure customers are informed about the breach within 24 hours.

Reassure stakeholders that corrective measures are being taken.

Minimize long-term reputational damage by demonstrating transparency and accountability.

3. Target Audiences

Identify the key stakeholders who need to be informed. Different messages may need to be crafted for different audiences, depending on their needs and the level of information they require.

Example:

Internal: Employees, Senior Leadership, IT Teams

External: Customers, Investors, Regulatory Authorities, Media

4. Key Messages

Develop the core messages that will be communicated to each audience. These should be concise, consistent, and adapted to the situation's specific circumstances.

Example Key Messages:

"We have identified and contained the breach."

"Your security is our top priority, and we are working closely with cybersecurity experts to safeguard your data."

"Customers affected will be provided with free credit monitoring services for a year."

5. Communication Channels

This section details how the messages will be delivered, whether through email, social media, press releases, or direct communication from leadership.

Example Channels:

Internal memos and staff meetings

Public press releases and website updates

Social media platforms (Twitter, LinkedIn)

Direct communication to customers via email

6. Spokespeople

Identify who will speak on behalf of the organization during the crisis. This ensures consistency in messaging and prevents unauthorized individuals from releasing potentially conflicting information.

Example:

CEO: Lead public spokesperson for media interviews.

Chief Information Officer (CIO): Technical spokesperson for detailed explanations of the breach.

Head of Public Relations: Responsible for managing day-to-day communications.

7. Timeline of Actions

This section outlines the timeline for key actions, ensuring that the right messages are sent out promptly and efficiently.

Example:

Day 1: Incident identified, internal communication sent, stakeholders informed.

Day 2: External press release, media interviews.

Day 3: Ongoing updates through social media, website, and email.

8. Follow-Up

After the immediate crisis has passed, it's essential to continue communicating with stakeholders, providing updates, and reassuring them of the organization's commitment to resolve the issue.

Example:

Weekly updates on the progress of internal investigations.

Continuous updates on new cybersecurity measures being implemented.

Appendix 2: Decision-Making Framework Template

When a crisis strikes, decisions need to be made quickly and effectively. This decision-making framework provides a step-by-step process for evaluating options, making informed decisions, and implementing them in a timely manner.

1. Define the Crisis

Clearly outline the nature of the crisis and the primary issue that needs to be addressed.

Example:

Crisis: Data breach affecting customer information.

Primary Issue: Protect customer data and prevent future breaches.

2. Identify Stakeholders

List all the individuals and groups impacted by the crisis. Consider their needs and how they should be involved in the decision-making process.

Example:

Stakeholders: Customers, employees, shareholders, regulators.

3. Assess the Impact

Evaluate the potential short-term and long-term impact of the crisis on the organization and its stakeholders. This step ensures decisions are made with a clear understanding of the consequences.

Example:

Short-term Impact: Loss of customer trust, potential regulatory fines.

Long-term Impact: Damage to brand reputation, financial losses, legal implications.

4. Generate Options

Brainstorm possible responses to the crisis, keeping in mind the needs of all stakeholders.

Example Options:

Option 1: Immediately disclose the breach to the public and offer compensation.

Option 2: Conduct an internal investigation first, then communicate findings.

Option 3: Hire external cybersecurity consultants to manage the breach and reassure customers.

5. Evaluate Risks and Benefits

Assess the risks and benefits associated with each option. This step ensures that leaders make balanced decisions based on both potential positive and negative outcomes.

Example Evaluation:

Option 1 Risk: May cause panic among customers.

Option 1 Benefit: Builds transparency and trust by being upfront.

6. Make the Decision

Choose the best course of action based on the evaluation of risks, benefits, and stakeholder needs.

Example: Opt for immediate disclosure combined with an external cybersecurity review to ensure transparency and customer reassurance.

7. Implement the Decision

Once the decision is made, execute it promptly. Assign roles and responsibilities for each step of the implementation process.

Example:

IT Department: Secure all systems, investigate breach.

PR Department: Prepare public statement.

Legal Team: Address regulatory requirements.

8. Review the Decision

After the crisis subsides, conduct a review to assess the effectiveness of the decision and identify lessons learned.

Appendix 3: Scenario Planning Template

Scenario planning prepares an organization for different potential crises by outlining various plausible situations and responses. This template provides a structured approach to developing scenarios and crafting detailed responses.

1. Identify Potential Scenarios

Start by brainstorming possible crisis situations that could affect your organization.

Example Scenarios:

- ✓ Cybersecurity breach.
- ✓ Natural disaster (e.g., earthquake affecting headquarters).
- ✓ Major product recall.

2. Develop a Detailed Narrative for Each Scenario

Write a detailed account of how the scenario could unfold, including possible causes, key stakeholders involved, and the likely impact on the organization.

Example:

- ✓ Scenario: Cybersecurity breach.
- ✓ Narrative: Hackers exploit a vulnerability in the company's software, gaining access to sensitive customer data, leading to widespread panic among stakeholders and media coverage.

3. Outline Key Actions

For each scenario, list the actions your organization would take in response. This includes both immediate and long-term actions.

Example Actions:

- ✓ Notify affected customers immediately.

- ✓ Engage cybersecurity experts to contain the breach.
- ✓ Conduct an internal audit to identify vulnerabilities.

4. Identify Key Stakeholders

List the stakeholders who would be involved or impacted in each scenario, along with the appropriate communication strategies.

Example Stakeholders:

- ✓ **Internal**: IT team, leadership, employees.
- ✓ **External**: Customers, media, regulatory bodies.

5. Review and Update Regularly

Scenario planning should be an ongoing process, with regular reviews and updates to keep the organization prepared for new or evolving threats.

Appendix 4: Post-Crisis Review Template

A post-crisis review is an essential tool for evaluating how a crisis was handled and identifying areas for improvement. This template guides organizations through a structured evaluation process.

1. Crisis Summary

Provide a brief summary of the crisis, including what happened, how it was addressed, and the outcome.

Example:

Crisis: Data breach affecting customer accounts.

Resolution: Issue contained within 48 hours; compensation offered to affected customers.

2. What Went Well

Identify the positive aspects of the crisis response. This includes actions that helped mitigate damage, stakeholder satisfaction, and quick decision-making.

Example:

The immediate involvement of external cybersecurity experts helped contain the breach.

Transparent communication with customers maintained trust.

3. Areas for Improvement

Highlight areas where the response could have been more effective. This may include communication breakdowns, delays in decision-making, or gaps in preparedness.

Example:

The company took too long to notify some customers, resulting in frustration.

IT security protocols were insufficient, requiring an overhaul.

4. Lessons Learned

Summarize the key lessons that the organization should take away from the crisis.

Example:

Improved cybersecurity measures must be put in place.

Faster, more efficient communication channels are needed during a crisis.

5. Action Plan

Develop a plan for implementing changes and improvements based on the lessons learned from the crisis.

Example Actions:

Invest in stronger cybersecurity infrastructure.

Conduct regular crisis response drills for all employees.

About the Author
'GERARD ASSEY'

Gerard Assey is a Graduate in Economics, a PGD in Management (HRD) and holds a Doctorate in Leadership. Gerard holds several International Qualifications in Sales, Debt Collection, Training & Teaching, and is a 'Fellow' of the prestigious 'Institute of Sales & Marketing Management'-UK, a Certified NLP Practitioner, a 'Certified Trainer', an 'Accredited Management Teacher-Behavioral Sciences', a 'Certified Competency Facilitator', a 'Certified Management Consultant'- (the International credentials of a professional management consultant, awarded in accordance with global standards of the ICMCI); and a Certification from the University of Michigan in 'Successful Negotiation: Essential Strategies and Skills'

He is also a Member of the 'National Association of Sales Professionals' backed with several years experience in varied industries, both in India and Overseas. He also holds an 'Etiquette Consultant' Certification from the USA (by Sue Fox, Author of Best Seller: 'Business Etiquette for Dummies'. She has trained some of the top celebrities' world over). He was also a recipient of a scholarship for extensive training in Japan on 'Corporate Management for India'.

Gerard Assey is 'Founder & Chief Corporate Trainer' of the Group: '**Citius, Altius, Fortius Unlimited**'- an organization that **celebrated 20 years of Glorious Service** in 2021, focusing on 3 Core Competencies:

People. Performance. Profit; in functional areas of Sales & Marketing, HR & Organizational Development, covering Recruitment, Training & Consultancy!

Having managed organizations with large Sales Forces in India & Overseas, his specialization cover extensive areas of Sales Training (All levels - Presentation, Negotiation, Key/ Strategic Accounts Management & Managerial Skills for all sectors), Bid Proposal/ Capture Planning/ Management Trainings, Retail Sales, Customer Service & Customer Retention Programs, Training for Prevention & Collection of Debt, Self & Personal Development Programs (Time Management, Teamwork & Team Building, Business Etiquette & Personal Grooming, Leadership & Managerial Skills, People Management Skills, Train-the-Trainer etc), including preparation of Custom-designed Business Manuals for Internal (HR, Induction, and Sales etc) & External use (Instruction, User Manuals).

Gerard has successfully conducted over 6470 Trainings & Workshops (as of July '25) all across India, Middle East, Africa, Europe & S.E. Asia. Besides public programs conducted regularly, both in India & Overseas, he has some of the top names as clients whom he services from Single Owners to large Public & Government undertakings, covering all sectors, for their in-house needs.

His website: www.CollectionSkills.com is the only one in this part of the world to be featured in the 'Collections & Credit Risk Magazine-USA' under 'Who's Who in Training' and ranks TOP, along with other websites listed below on most search engines.

Gerard is author of 202 books already (Aug 2025), all the books being available on all online platforms and outlets as E-books and Paperbacks

A few of our business related books:

1. Bite-sized Bits on Commonsense Management
2. Heart to Heart on Life's Principles'
3. How to become a Successful Manager
4. The Sales Professionals' Master Workbook of S.Y.S.T.E.M.S
5. The Professional Business Email Etiquette Handbook & Guide
6. The Professional Business Video-Conferencing Etiquette Handbook & Guide
7. Professional Presentation Skills
8. Exceptional Customer Service
9. Professional Tele-Marketing Skills
10. Professional Debt Collection Skills
11. The G.R.E.A.T. Sales & Service Workbook
12. Sales Training Advantage for Results (*The Ultimate Sales Training Manual to enable you stand out as a S.T.A.R.*)
13. CEO Daily Planner & Organizer
14. The Sales Professionals' Master Daily Planner
15. The Professional Debt Collector's Master Daily Planner
16. My Daily Planner & Organizer
17. MY EMERGENCY INFORMATION RECORD (Family Emergency & Peace of Mind Planner)
18. The Ultimate Therapist & Counselors Planner and Organizer
19. Building an Ethical Workplace
20. Managing Relationships at Work
21. Managing Business Meetings Effectively
22. Effective Delegation Skills
23. Goal Setting for Success
24. B2B Selling by Email
25. Professional Business Etiquette & Grooming
26. Dining Etiquette & Table Manners
27. Effective Networking Skills
28. Grooming, Etiquette & Manners for Teens, Young Adults & Future Leaders
29. Inter-Personal Skills
30. Get Ready, Get Hired!
31. Selling in a Recession
32. Effective Receivables Management in an Economic Downturn!
33. Real Estate & Property Sales Training
34. Credit Sales & Accounts Receivable Management

35. Selling Skills for Real Estate & Property Advisors
36. Take G.R.E.A.T. C.A.R.E!
37. Spa, Salon & Health Club Selling Skills
38. Selling Travel, Holiday & MICE Services
39. Selling Skills for Spa's, Salons & Health Clubs
40. Retailing in Salons & Spas
41. Selling Holiday, Vacation, Tours & Packages
42. The Power of Sales Referrals
43. Selling Luxury
44. Technical Selling Skills
45. Financial Advisors Sales Training
46. Dealing with Burnout at Work Monopolize Your Markets
47. Selling to Affluent Customers
48. Growing up with Grace
49. Financial Selling Skills
50. *The Effective Manager's Guide: Key Skills to Thrive*
51. From Aspiring to Inspiring: A Guide for New Managers on the Rise
52. The Power of Focus
53. Selling with Integrity: Sell Like Jesus The Perfect Role Model!
54. 31 Habits of Champions: Your 31-Day Journey to Greatness
55. Rejecting Grasshopper Talk: From Grasshopper to Giant-Killer-*Defeating Giants Daily!*
56. Navigate the AI-Powered Future of Bid & Proposals: Up-Skill to Stay Relevant with Alternative Career Paths & Opportunities
57. Hiring Sales Winners
58. Present with Impact
59. Success Unlocked: *Breaking Free from Habits that Hold You Back*
60. Complaints to Cheers, Feedback to Gold: Mastering Complaints Management
61. Thriving Together: *Cultivating Diversity, Equity, and Inclusion*
62. Coaching Skills for Sales Managers
63. Soaring to Success in Business & Leadership: Swifter, Higher, Stronger!
64. From Classroom to Podium: A Student's Guide to Powerful Public Speaking & Presentation Skills
65. Developing Self-Discipline
66. The CEO's 31-Day Power Plan: Unlocking Success through Essential Traits

67. Credibility Matters
68. A Winning Attitude
69. Bid & Proposal Management Using AI
70. Sales Forecasting: A Practical & Proven Guide to Strategic Sales Forecasting
71. Elevate & Energize: *50 Dynamic & Fun Activities for Peak Workplace Morale*
72. 'Sales SOS! Sales on Fire! *30 Days to Conquer Chaos & the Nightmares of Success!'*
73. Mastering Sales Managerial Skills: *Building High-Performing Teams & Driving Exceptional Results*
74. Eagle-Eyed Leadership: Unleashing the Power of 31 Lessons from Eagles
75. The Ultimate Employee Training Guide: *Training Today, Leading Tomorrow*
76. Being More Accountable at Work
77. Creating a Culture of Continuous Improvement
78. Effective Questioning & Listening Skills
79. The Power of Value Selling
80. The Growth Mindset
81. Mastering Professional Help Desk Skills
82. The Power to Lead with Empathy
83. Being Prepared: The Key to Unlocking Success
84. Youthful Spark-Youth Energizers, Activities and Games-Igniting the Fun in Youth
85. Ignite your Motivation for Success
86. Elevate Your Executive Presence: *Your Roadmap to Executive Excellence*
87. Smart Decisions: *Mastering Problem Solving with Strategic Solutions for Business Success*
88. Strategic Planning: *Developing and Implementing Strategic Plans to Achieve Long-Term Business Goals*
89. The Power of Stay Interviews
90. Developing G.R.I.T.
91. Adaptability
92. Diagnosis- *A Key Skill for Leadership*
93. The Burnout-Proof Salesperson: *The Master Guide to Preventing Stress & Burnout-* Strategies for Thriving in Sales
94. Learning from Failure: *Keys to Success*
95. Customer Success Management
96. Overcoming the Killers of Motivation
97. The C-Suite Code: *Mastering Skills for Executive Excellence'*

98. Dealing with Difficult Customers
99. Unlocking Your Potential: Mastering the Top 20 Life Skills for a Brighter Future
100. Nurturing Tomorrow's Leaders: *Essential Soft Skills Every Child Must Learn*
101. Lively & Fun Party Games for Seniors & Elders
102. Role Playing for Sales Champions: From Practice to Performance
103. Fun and Exciting Party Games for Kids
104. Case Studies for Sales
105. Role-Playing for Unbeatable Customer Service
106. Case Studies in Customer Service
107. Case Studies in Winning Negotiations
108. Case Studies in Management & Leadership
109. Case Studies in Human Resources & Talent Management
110. CEO Success Blueprint: The Essential Toolkit for CEOs and C-Level Executives
111. The Salesperson's Self-Coaching Guide: *Master Your Own Self-Coaching Plan for Success*
112. Overcoming Procrastination: *Your Ultimate Guide to Stop Delaying and Start Living Your Best Life*
113. When True Colors Are Exposed: *The Journey to Unmasking Humanity*
114. Life-Changing Habits for Teens: Teen Success Blueprint for a Bright Future
115. Workplace Stress-Free: *Proven Strategies to Thrive at Work and Beyond*
116. Objection Overruled: *The Ultimate Guide to Turning 'No' into 'Yes'"*
117. Building Strong Teams: *A Comprehensive Guide to Team Building*
118. Ethical & Moral Leadership in Business: *Eliminating Unethical Practices & Building a Culture of Trust & Integrity*
119. Rising Strong: Building Positive: High Self-Esteem for a Fulfilling Life-*A Practical Guide for Students, Employees, Leaders & Entrepreneurs*
120 The Cheerful Mindset: Cultivating a Joyful Outlook Everyday
121. Leading Through Crisis: Case Studies on Crisis Management

Besides regularly contributing to business & trade journals, including international ones such as the 'Creative Training Techniques' and the 'Sales News' of the U.S.A, He is also a member of several prestigious bodies & trade associations, having participated in many Conferences & Workshops in India & Overseas.

Prior to his last assignment of leading & managing a large MNC as head, Gerard had a 3-year stint in the Middle East as a Consultant with a leading British Consultancy Firm.

As the past 'Official Country Representative' for the International Business Award- 'THE STEVIES'-(the business world's own Oscar) for about 4 years- he ensured a few Indian companies that qualify for the same every year!

Gerard can be contacted at:
Email: training@Sales-Training.in,training@CollectionSkills.com
Websites:

www.Sales-Training.in
www.EtiquetteWorks.in
www.CollectionSkills.com
www.RetailSalesTraining.in
www.SalesTrainingIndia.com
www.ManualPreparation.com
www.TrainingWithPuppets.com
www.FirstContactAcademy.com
www.SalesAndMarketingRecruiter.com

Our TRAININGS that can help your team

- ✓ **Sales Effectiveness**: Selling Skills for any Sector: Service/ Logistics/ FMCG Realty/ Insurance & Finance/ Media/ SPA's, Health Clubs & Salons/ Key Account Management, Effective Negotiation Skills/ Bid & Proposal Management Skills/ Retail Sales Training: Any Sector (Auto, Jewelry, Clothing, Luxury etc)
- ✓ **Customer Service Skills**-Complaints Handling & Customer Retention
- ✓ **Debt Prevention & Collection Skills**
- ✓ **Etiquette & Grooming**
- ✓ **Leadership & Managerial Skills**
- ✓ **Self & Personal Development Skills**: Presentation Skills/ Effective Communication Skills/Business Proposal Writing Skills/ Problem Solving & Decision Making Skills/ Empowering Secretaries-The perfect PA! (For Secretaries & PA's)/ Effective Time Management/ Teamwork & Teambuilding/ P.R.I.D.E- **P**ersonal **R**esponsibility **I**n **D**elivering **E**xcellence

www.ingramcontent.com/pod-product-compliance
Ingram Content Group UK Ltd.
Pitfield, Milton Keynes, MK11 3LW, UK
UKHW021339190726
13845UKWH00027B/623

9 788198 926203